Keeping Covenant with the Lord in the
Seven Mountains of Culture - Book Two

Covenant & Family

Keeping Covenant with the Lord in the
Seven Mountains of Culture - Book Two

Covenant & Family

Rivkah Isaacs

Treasures of Glory Ministries
SAN DIEGO, CA

PUBLISHED BY TREASURES OF GLORY MINISTRIES
P.O. Box 23743, San Diego, CA 92193-3743
www.treasuresofglory.com

ISBN: 978-0-9916112-4-9

To all families who diligently seek
keeping the covenant of the Lord

TABLE OF CONTENTS

PREFACE

"Covenant & Family" continues this series, "Keeping Covenant with the Lord in the Seven Mountains of Culture." Each book contains prayers of repentance pertaining to how we as members of the Royal Priesthood and citizens of the United States of America have broken covenant with the Lord in the seven mountains of culture. If you are a citizen from another country, you are invited to join in these prayers for your nation as well.

These prayers and the biblical principles applied in this series was birthed during my role as the National Prayer Team Leader for The 2016 Committee—Formerly the National Draft Ben Carson for President Committee. Our focus was to pray according to 2 Chronicles 7:14:

> *"If My people who are called by My name will humble themselves, and pray and seek My face, and turn from their wicked ways, then I will hear from heaven, and will forgive their sin and heal their land."*

As we sought the Lord in prayer for repentance of our personal sins, the sins of our generations, and those of our nation, the Lord continued to take us into deeper areas of repentance that led us to repenting of breaking covenant with Him as a nation in the seven mountains of culture.

The teachings on the seven mountains of culture bring to light the areas that impact every nation: religion, family, economy, government, arts/entertainment, media and education. Each of these mountains shapes the culture based on the role they play in each particular nation. Because of this understanding of culture, many believers seek ways to influence these seven areas in order to bring revival to the nations. This series brings another aspect of healing to these areas of culture that impact the nations. Please, feel free to further your study on the seven mountains of culture if this is of interest to you. However, additional research is not necessary to follow along with the prayers in this series.

INTRODUCTION:
HOW TO USE THIS BOOK

I INVITE YOU ON A JOURNEY that leads along the narrow path of repentance of the sins of us as individuals, our previous generations, and of our nation in order to lead us to the Lord's forgiveness and healing of our land (2 Chr 7:14; Matt 7:13-14; Ps 18:19). In accordance with the seven mountains of culture, we continue with the mountain of family as we focus on bringing healing to our nation beginning with our role as members of the Royal Priesthood in Yeshua HaMashiach, Jesus Christ.

COVENANT

As I CONTINUE TO STUDY THE BIBLE, the more I see it is written from the perspective of covenant. Everything God includes in the Bible comes from the aspect of covenant. He outlines what behavior allows us to remain in covenant with Him in order to access the fullness of the blessings and provisions of His covenant. In addition, the Lord details what behaviors are not acceptable and the consequences that follow when we do not obey His instructions. Since He is a good God, He wants us to live from the blessings of the covenant. When we disobey, the Lord our Redeemer has made provision for reconciliation with Him so we may walk in right relationship with Him.

3

We live in a society where contracts and agreements are at the forefront, while the concept of covenant is not given much thought. Perhaps we are used to the current day culture of contracts and the fine print of companies who sell a product or a service who intend to hold back benefits and customer service in order to not fully grant the buyer the full satisfaction of the purchase. A transaction of this sort needs to be life giving to both the company that sells it, as well as the customer. Those who provide the product or service do indeed need to make a profit. Likewise, the customer's life should be enhanced by the purchase of the item. How many times are items or services purchased where the focus of the best interest is fully on the part of the company selling that passes along costs to the buyer that go beyond the purchase price?

Another aspect that delineates between covenant and contracts is that covenants are made based in trust, and contracts are made based on mistrust. When the Lord makes a covenant with us, it is binding and comes from a place of love and faithfulness on His part. We hinder our covenant relationship with Him when we think the covenant is to force or control God or us to satisfy the terms as is the case with the mistrust that compels the need for contracts.

Living in covenant relationship with the Lord of Hosts includes no fine print. He discloses all the benefits and blessings pertaining to covenant that come from obeying Him. In fact, the Lord takes pleasure in satisfying the covenant He has made with us. Yeshua/Jesus speaks to His disciples from a covenant perspective when He says:

> *"And do not seek what you should eat or what you should drink, nor have an anxious mind. For all these things the nations of the world seek after, and your Father knows that you need these*

things. But seek the kingdom of God, and all these things shall be added to you.

"Do not fear, little flock, for it is your Father's good pleasure to give you the kingdom" (Luke 12:29-32).

Yeshua/Jesus tells His disciples that it is the Father's good pleasure to give us the Kingdom. What wonderful news! Being given the Kingdom can only be accomplished through covenant relationship with the Lord. And, living in covenant relationship requires action and obedience fully disclosed in the pages of Scripture.

As members of the Royal Priesthood, we must come into agreement and grow in understanding of living in covenant with the Lord of Hosts. Since the main focus of this book and series is living in covenant with the Lord, if you are not familiar with the concept of covenant, I encourage you to explore this topic further. Much information on covenant can be found at Christian bookstores or through Internet searches.

Covenant & Nations

The United States of America was founded on Judeo/Christian beliefs, as well as a covenant to the Lord made by President George Washington. Since we have entered into a covenant with the Lord on a national level, when we sin as a nation, we break covenant with Him. This book, and the ones to follow in this series, will focus on how we can bring healing to our nation in these areas by repenting of sins recorded in the Bible as they pertain to each of the seven mountains relating to living in covenant with the Lord of Hosts. If you are a citizen of another nation, you are welcome to join in prayers of repentance and replacement for the healing of your nation.

God made an everlasting covenant with Abraham and his descendants, which includes the land (Gen 17:7). Where Israel is the only nation where the Lord initiated the covenant with a people, it is not the only nation who has chosen to enter into covenant with the Lord. In addition to the United States of America, examples of nations who made a covenant with the Lord of Hosts include, but are not limited to, Armenia and Australia.

This book's premise of repentance is in the context of a nation being in covenant with the Lord. However, if you reside in a nation whose government has not entered into a covenant with the Lord, you are encouraged to modify these prayers to repent of sinning against the Lord as a nation—as your nation would be guilty of these sins—but not guilty of breaking covenant with the Lord. Another point to take into consideration would be whether or not the leaders of your nation entered into covenant with Satan and/or the kingdom of darkness. If so, you may decide it best to repent on behalf of your nation for keeping covenant with the Enemy by committing the sins listed in each section. More information of repentance on behalf of your nation will be explained shortly.

HOW TO USE THIS BOOK

EACH CHAPTER OF THIS BOOK contains six sections: *Repentance, Replacement, Forgiveness, Blessing Israel, Stewardship & Growth in Spiritual Authority* and *Blessing*. Each of these sections are described below that detail the biblical principles applied, as well as how to use each section.

Applying biblical principles to praying for the healing of our nation is strategic and increases the effectiveness of our prayers, time and energy expended. Each of the principles listed presents an action and guarantees a positive result in the execution of the positive action.

As you continue with the next sections, I invite you to take a look ahead at a couple of chapters. In doing so, the instructions immediately following will make more sense in context of the chapters.

Depending on the flow of each chapter, sometimes the repentance and replacement sections are separate, while other times they are combined. Feel free to separate or combine them as works best for you.

Some topics may be easier to go through, while other may be more difficult due to the areas of repentance the Lord highlights in your life. You may want to have your journal handy, or one that is set aside for this book to keep track of the Lord ministering to you as you seek Him. The sections on *Stewardship & Growth in Spiritual Authority* include questions that facilitate reflection and steps for implementation of strategies that you may find helpful to keep in written form.

REPENTANCE

"If My people who are called by My name will humble themselves, and pray and seek My face, and turn from their wicked ways, then I will hear from heaven, and will forgive their sin and heal their land."
—2 CHRONICLES 7:14

AS WE DELVE INTO THE DIFFERENT THEMES of repentance and replacement for each chapter, we deal specifically with sins that result in negative actions. When dealing with specific sins, we increase our effectiveness because we recognize something is sin, take responsibility for it, repent of it, remove it and replace with a right action or change in thinking. In doing so, we engage in prayers to the Lord that are precise and effective. For example praying to the Lord, "Please forgive us of our iniquities," is not an effective or precise prayer, even though it may be well intended. It is vague and takes no responsibility for particular sins. Also, there is then no specific focus with repentance with regards to changing behavior and way of thinking. However, "Lord, please forgive us of the pride of power," is a specific and strategic prayer. It shows acknowledgment of the sin, which leads to taking responsibility of the sin, and then gives opportunity for us to put into action a plan for replacing that sin with a positive behavior. Please remember that repentance can include acts of commission, things we have done; or acts of omission, things we have not done.

Second Chronicles chapter seven explains a biblical principle of repentance of the people of the Lord resulting in forgiveness of sin and healing of the land. Humility, prayer, seeking the face of the Lord and turning from wicked ways describe the principles that lead to forgiveness of sins and the healing to be received from the Lord. In keeping with this principle found in 2 Chronicles 7:14, we will repent of breaking covenant with the Lord relating to our individual role as members of the Royal Priesthood, in our generations and as a nation.

Repenting comprises the following: recognizing the sin, taking responsibility for the sin, repenting of the sin and turning away from repeating the sin. Repentance involves more that just being sorry for doing something wrong. It involves changing our mind, no longer committing the negative action and replacing with a right action. The Greek word [G3340] translated as "repent" means, "to change one's mind, i.e. to repent; to change one's mind for better, heartily to amend with abhorrence of one's past sins." Keeping in alignment with this definition, the sins we repent of will be followed by asking the Lord to replace them with a right action, and/or replacing with the nature and character of Yeshua HaMashiach, Jesus Christ.

Individual repentance comes prior to repenting for our generations or on behalf our nation, as we need to first take the plank out of our own eye before removing the speck from our brother's eye. There are many sins listed that each of us have not committed personally. However, since we are looking to repent of the sins of our generations and those of our nation, it is best to begin with personal repentance. In doing so, we are clean before the Lord and then have the authority to repent on behalf of our generations and our nation. By repenting first of individual sins, we can then pray to repent for our generations and nation from a place of humility, not from judgment or pride.

The Bible speaks of generational sins being passed down in the family line in several passages (Ex 20:5; Ex 34:7; Num 14:18; Deut 5:9). We can accomplish repentance of these generational sins and the sins of our forefathers as recorded in Nehemiah 1:6 and 9:2. By repenting of the sins of our generations, we can break the generational propensity to be held captive by the effects of these sins. Repentance of generational sins that our families made that contributed to the sins of our nation grants us greater spiritual authority when repenting on behalf of the sins of our nation.

Scripture references to repentance on behalf of the sins on a national level are found in Daniel chapter nine and Nehemiah chapters one and nine. Repentance on behalf of the nation may also be referred to as identificational repentance. When we repent on behalf of the sins of our nation, we repent and identify as though we committed the sin and ask the Lord's forgiveness. Daniel gives a good example of this in his prayer recorded in chapter nine.

REPLACEMENT

Do not be overcome by evil,
but overcome evil with good.
—ROMANS 12:21

AFTER REPENTANCE, our focus turns to replacement and overcoming evil with good. Scripture is a weapon against the enemy. Yeshua/Jesus used it when tempted by the devil. However, we need to understand what verses are to be used as warfare and which ones give insight as how to live or have the nature of God that results in effective warfare. When we focus on the replacement aspect in each chapter, our purpose is to replace with the nature and character of the Lord based on the truth found in Scripture.

The replacement items come from verses that are in the opposite spirit of the sin we repented of on behalf of ourselves, our generations and our nation. When removing a negative action or sin, we advance to zero. In order to have leverage to be victorious over the sin we repented of and removed, we need to replace with a positive or a right action, bringing us into positive numbers. For example, when repenting of and removing fear, we need the perfect love of the Lord that casts out fear to be the replacement for the fear (1 John 4:18). It is not the verse about perfect love that casts out fear, it is perfect love that does so.

Another example of a Scripture that is a principle for both repentance and replacement comes from 2 Chronicles 7:14. This verse gives us step-by-step instructions for the Lord's forgiveness and healing of the land. Memorizing and reciting this verse in prayer alone is not the purpose of this passage, nor is it effective warfare. Remember, just knowing and memorizing Scripture does not guarantee transformation into godly character. Satan and many of the religious leaders recorded in the Bible knew Scripture very well. Yeshua/Jesus spoke strong words concerning the hypocrisy of knowing the Word but not living it. Scripture memorization and recitation without application and transformation is dangerous deceptive and destructive. Therefore, replacement in this book means that we apply the Word of the Lord in our lives in order to be continually transformed into the nature and character of the Lord revealed to us in His Word.

FORGIVENESS

"And forgive us our debts,
As we forgive our debtors."
—MATTHEW 6:12

"For if you forgive men their trespasses,
your heavenly Father will also forgive you.
But if you do not forgive men their trespasses,
neither will your Father forgive your trespasses."
—MATTHEW 6:14-15

FORGIVENESS FOLLOWS ON THE HEELS of repentance and replacement in order that we may be forgiven by the Father for the sins of which we repented. Yeshua/Jesus speaks directly to the importance of forgiving others. We will only be forgiven of our sins if we forgive the sins of those who sin against us. If at any point we want to see if another angle or loophole exists that releases us from forgiving others in order to be forgiven ourselves, it does not exist. Forgiving others in order to be forgiven is recorded in five passages in eight different verses. As we see in the verse above from Matthew 6:14-15, Yeshua/Jesus gives both the positive results of forgiveness, as well as the negative consequence of not forgiving others.

BLESS ISRAEL

"I will bless those who bless you,
And I will curse him who curses you;
And in you all the families of the earth shall be blessed."
—GENESIS 12:3

AS WE SEEK HEALING FOR OUR NATION through repentance, replacement and forgiving others, we can increase our effectiveness by implementing another biblical principle of blessing Israel and the Jews. God promises that He will bless those who bless the descendants of Abraham; and that He will curse those who curse them. This promise seems to include blessings that extend beyond the law of sowing and reaping—more on the subject of sowing and reaping to follow.

Isaiah reveals that a nation who does not serve Jerusalem shall perish and be utterly ruined:

"For the nation and kingdom which will not serve you shall perish,
And those nations shall be utterly ruined" (Isaiah 60:12).

We can serve Israel by standing alongside, supporting and praying for her. In order to remain as a nation, we need to come into agreement with Scripture in order that we may continue to exist. There are many sins that need to be repented of and turned away from in our nation. However, based on the Word, it seems that if we stand in agreement with Israel, the Lord's blessing and mercy may be extended to grant us more time to for the healing and restoration of our nation even if other wrong actions have yet to be righted. For example, if we do not stand with Israel and we get the abortion law overturned, as important as not killing the life of the unborn child is, it will not exempt us from the judgment of the Lord for not standing with Israel.

When we bless God's people with the replacement verses, we activate yet another biblical principle found in the law of sowing and reaping:

Do not be deceived, God is not mocked; for whatever a man sows,
that he will also reap (Galatians 6:7).

Utilizing the law of sowing and reaping seems to be in addition to the blessings that come from the Lord by blessing the Jews. If we want to increase in receiving blessings and growing in the nature and character of the Lord, an effective way to accomplish this comes through blessing others in the areas we want to acquire. Reaping is specific to what we sow. Therefore, being specific and strategic in how we bless Israel and the Jews based on our replacement topics not only helps them, but helps us as well.

You may be wondering, "What about blessing other nations? Don't we want to bless them as well?" Yes, we do want all nations to be blessed. In blessing Israel we bless all the nations, for the Lord purposes that the descendants of Abraham and the nation of Israel be a blessing to the families and nations of the earth (Gen 18:18; Gen 22:18; Gen 26:4).

Each chapter contains a prayer to bless Israel relating to the replacement verses from the Old Testament. In honoring the Jews' faith in God and believing that the Messiah is still to be revealed, none of our prayers for Israel or the Jews are offered in the name of Jesus. We can still pray to the Lord and ask His blessing on the Jews in a way that remains true to our beliefs as followers of Yeshua/Jesus, while at the same time respecting the beliefs of our Jewish brothers and sisters.

STEWARDSHIP & GROWTH IN SPIRITUAL AUTHORITY

"'Well done, good and faithful servant; you were faithful over a few things, I will make you ruler over many things.'"
—MATTHEW 25:21

But he who looks into the perfect law of liberty and continues in it, and is not a forgetful hearer but a doer of the work, this one will be blessed in what he does.
—JAMES 1:25

AS THOROUGH AND IMPORTANT as the prayers of repentance, replacement and forgiveness may be, our task of overcoming evil with good does not end with these. Victory in overcoming evil with good can only be gained by putting it into practice. We are to be good stewards with the knowledge the Lord has given to us. Therefore, each chapter provides an opportunity to apply biblical principles of stewardship that will facilitate further growth and blessing.

Please take time with the Father and ask Him the questions in order that you may continue to increase in your ability to live from the blessings and provision of the covenant of life and peace. Questions involve taking a look at actions or thoughts that need to be removed, as well as adding in positive behaviors or responses. These questions correspond with the theme of repentance and replacement. You may find it helpful to write down your answers in a separate journal of your choosing or the journal designed to accompany this book, which is sold separately.

In order to keep the momentum of removing, replacing and growing in stewardship in these areas in your life, you may find it encouraging working through this book with a trusted friend or prayer group.

Blessing

Death and life are in the power of the tongue,
And those who love it will eat its fruit.
—Proverbs 18:21

Another aspect of replacement that we apply in each chapter includes blessings. Many passages of Scripture contain blessings and speak to the impact they have on those receiving them. The tongue has within it the power of life and death. Life from blessing and death from cursing are exemplified over again in both the Old and New Testaments.

Each chapter closes with a blessing that incorporates the replacement verses for that topic. Speaking words of blessings from these verses contain the power to give life. You may choose to read the blessing out loud or quietly to yourself. In addition, you may have opportunity to read the blessings over others.

The Scriptural Foundation for Blessings

Blessings are spoken of and given in both the Old and New Testaments. The most commonly used Hebrew word for "bless" [H1288] means, "to bless." The English word "bless" means: "(1) To pronounce a wish of happiness to one; to express a wish or desire of happiness. Genesis 28:1; (2) to make happy; to make successful; to prosper in temporal concerns; as, we are blest with peace and plenty. Deuteronomy 15:4."

Scripture includes blessings from God to people, from people to God, and from people to people. Included below contains a list of a sampling of verses pertaining to blessings.

Examples of God blessing people: Genesis 12:3; Genesis 26:3; Exodus 20:24; Psalm 5:2; Psalm 29:11

Examples of people blessing God: Psalm 16:7; Psalm 18:46; Psalm 89:52; 2 Corinthians 1:3

Examples of fathers blessing their sons: Genesis 27:1-4; Genesis 28:1; Genesis 48

Example of one person blessing another: Genesis 24:60; Ruth 4:11-12; 1 Samuel 26:25; Psalm 41:1; Psalm 128:1-6; Luke 2:34-33; James 1:12

Blessings others is a command: Matthew 5:44; Luke 6:27-28; John 13:35; Romans 12:14; James 1:12; James 3:1-11

God acknowledges blessings from people to people: Genesis 12:3

Phrases used for blessings:
May you become (Genesis 24:60)
I bless… (Genesis 48:9)
May the Lord God … and bless you (Deuteronomy 1:11)
The Lord make…(Ruth 4:11-12)
The Lord bless you (Psalm 128:5)

DEFINITIONS

Family: In order to keep things streamlined, the traditional words for family members are used throughout this book. If you were raised in a foster family situation, please apply the term to the relationships as they best fit your situation. The same goes for living in blended families and any other combination of family relationships as they pertain to you.

Jew: To many Christians, it seems disrespectful to use the term "Jew," as it has been used disparagingly over the last couple hundred years. However, the term is not disrespectful as it came into use after the dispersion to refer to those from the kingdom of Judah or land of Judea—"Jew" is a shortened version of "Judah" or "Judea." Both terms of "Jew" and "Jewish people" are used interchangeably throughout this book to refer to the descendants of Abraham, Isaac and Jacob.

Yeshua: In Hebrew, the correct translation for the name of the Messiah is "Yeshua," which means, "salvation" [H3444]. The name "Yeshua" does not translate correctly to Jesus in Greek, Latin or English. Most English translations of Matthew 1:21 say something similar to this:

"And she will bring forth a Son, and you shall call His name Jesus,
  for He will save His people from their sins."

Not understanding the context of the Hebrew word for salvation, this verse does not make sense as to why He would be called Jesus. It does make sense when Yeshua, meaning salvation,s is used in place of Jesus.

Another Hebrew term used in relation to Yeshua is "HaMashiach." In Hebrew, "Ha" means "the" and "Mashiach" means "Messiah." Therefore, Yeshua HaMashiach is used in this book in connection with the name Jesus Christ.

Both the Hebrew and English names for Yeshua HaMashiach and the Lord Jesus Christ are used interchangeably throughout this book.

PART 1

COVENANT IN FAMILY

But the mercy of the LORD is from everlasting to everlasting
On those who fear Him,
And His righteousness to children's children,
To such as keep His covenant,
And to those who remember His commandments to do them.
—PSALM 103:17-18

THE EVERLASTING MERCY OF THE LORD is on those who fear Him, and He gives generational blessings to those who keep His covenant and follow His commandments. Therefore, it is essential that we keep covenant with the Lord in our families. In doing so, generational blessings are poured out to the children's children of those who keep His covenant. Family is the foundation and building block of our society. Everything flows out from the family, to society and up to government. When families are strong and keep covenant with the Lord, then so does the rest of society.

In taking a closer look at Psalm 103:18, the Hebrew word [H8104] translated as "keep" means, "to keep, guard, observe, and give heed." When we keep the covenant of the Lord, we are to not only keep the commandments and instructions of the Lord that pertain to the covenant, but we are to guard and protect the covenant. Just as a marriage covenant needs to be kept, guarded and protected, so does the covenant we have with the Lord and how it pertains to our families.

These next few chapters cover repentance of not keeping, guarding and protecting covenant in our families. As we repent, we will include areas of replacement. The Lord intends for you to live victoriously in your family. In order to do so, you will need to overcome the evil that has been removed with the goodness found in the nature of God and in His Word.

Beginning with repentance of behalf of ourselves for how we have sinned pertaining to those things entrusted to us from the Lord allows us to increase our authority over other areas in our sphere of influence, including our influence for our government. When we are faithful in few things, the Lord gives us increasingly greater responsibility and increases our sphere of influence. Jesus teaches how this works in the Kingdom of Heaven in the parable of the talents (Matthew 25:14-30). This parable about the Kingdom of Heaven directly relates to how the Lord operates His Kingdom on earth. The master in the parable says, "well done," to the servants who were faithful over a few things. He then makes them a ruler over many things. Likewise, as we are faithful in covenant relationship to the Lord in our families, He will increase our authority beyond the scope of the immediate family.

Chapter 1

COVENANT IN FAMILY #1

"But as for me and my house, we will serve the LORD."
—JOSHUA 24:15

REPENTANCE

"Hear, O Israel: The LORD our God, the Lord is one! You shall love the Lord your God with all your heart, with all your soul, and with all your strength. And these words which I command you today shall be in your heart. You shall teach them diligently to your children, and shall talk of them when you sit in your house, when you walk by the way, when you lie down, and when you rise up."
—DEUTERONOMY 6:4-7

AS A MEMBER OF THE ROYAL PRIESTHOOD, please repent for not keeping covenant with the Lord by breaking covenant in the family on behalf of yourself, your generations and your nation, and on behalf of your nation for the following:

- not serving the Lord as a family (Josh 24:15)
- not loving the Lord with all your heart, soul and strength (Deut 6:4-7)
- not teaching your children to love the Lord with all their heart, soul and strength (Deut 6:4-7)
- not teaching your children to obey the commandments of the Lord (Deut 6:4-7)

- not living in unity with the Father, Son and Holy Spirit and not living in unity as a family (John 17:20-23)
- committing adultery and fornication (Ex 20:14; Gal 5:19)
- divorcing in the event of hardness of heart (Matt 19:8)
  - In the event of adultery in marriage, the covenant was broken prior to the divorce. In these cases, divorce is the legal dissolution of a broken covenant relationship. Also, I am not advocating that people remain in abusive marriages. In these cases, the adultery and abuse are covenant breakers and need to be repented of as such.
- implementing improper discipline or instruction
  - being too lenient (Prov 13:24)
  - being too harsh and provoking your children to wrath (Eph 6:4)
- dishonoring your father and mother (Ex 20:12)
- choosing not to provide for your family (1 Tim 5:8)
- not taking care of the welfare, health or safety of your family members
  - The Lord makes a covenant of peace with you as a member of the Royal Priesthood (Is 54:10; Ez 34:25; Ez 37:26; Mal 2:5). The Hebrew word [H7965] translated as peace is shalom. Shalom includes definitions of "welfare, health and safety." When these are willfully not provided for in a family, the parents violate the covenant to their family that the Lord has entrusted to them.
- committing abortion (Ex 20:13; Ps 106:38-41; Prov 6:16-17)
  - Abortion breaks covenant with the unborn child. In covenant, parents are to protect their children.

Please repent of the list above on behalf of yourself, your generations and your nation as to how you have hurt others by these actions.

Replacement

As a member of the Royal Priesthood, please replace with the following:

- *choosing to serve the Lord as a family (Josh 24:15)*
- *loving the Lord with all your heart, soul and strength (Deut 6:4-7)*
- *teaching your children to love the Lord with all their heart, soul and strength (Deut 6:4-7)*
- *teaching your children to obey the commandments of the Lord (Deut 6:4-7)*
- *living in unity with the Father, Son and Holy Spirit and not living in unity as a family (John 17:20-23)*
- *husband loving wife as he loves himself; wife respecting husband (Eph 5:33)*
- *being faithful to husband/wife (Ex 20:14; Heb 13:4)*
- *abstaining from sexual immorality (1 Thess 4:3-5; 2 Tim 2:22)*
- *having a clean heart (Ps 51:10)*
- *giving proper discipline and instruction (Duet 6:6-7; Prov 13:24; Prov 22:6; Eph 6:4; Col 3:21)*
- *honoring father and mother (Ex 20:12)*
- *choosing to provide for family (1 Tim 5:8)*
- *taking care of the welfare, health or safety of family members*
- *believing and living from the truth that children are a blessing from the Lord (Ps 127:3; Ps 139:13-15)*

Forgiveness

I choose to forgive from my heart, (person's name), for how he/she did not keep covenant of the Lord in the family by (fill in from list below), which caused injury to myself and/or my loved ones, either now or in the past.

- not serving the Lord as a family
- not loving the Lord with all his/her heart, soul and strength
- not teaching children to love the Lord with all their heart, soul and strength
- not teaching children to obey the commandments of the Lord
- not living in unity with the Father, Son and Holy Spirit and not living in unity as a family
- committing adultery and/or fornication
- divorcing in the event of hardness of heart
- disciplining children inappropriately
- being too lenient in disciplining children
- being too harsh and provoking children to wrath
- dishonoring father and mother
- choosing not to provide for family
- not taking care of the welfare, health or safety of family members
- having an abortion, attempting an abortion, helping with an abortion, etc.

Bless Israel

Dear Heavenly Father, thank You for Your covenant of peace You have with Israel. I bless Israel and her families with Your shalom. Please give all Israeli and all Jewish parents the courage, strength and wisdom needed to raise their children in Your ways according to the Torah—the law and instruction in the Old Testament. Please bless Israel with Your love for them as their Father, amen.

STEWARDSHIP & GROWTH
IN SPIRITUAL AUTHORITY

DEAR HEAVENLY FATHER, thank You for the covenant of peace You made with me. Please show me how I am to live from this covenant of peace within my family.

- What am I doing that I need to change, eliminate or do differently in light of what I have repented of in my life and generations?

- What do I need as far as resources, training, etc. in order for me to make the needed adjustments?
- How would You like me to implement the changes?

- How can I bless my family this week from the covenant of peace You have with me?

BLESSING

BELOVED, YOU ARE CREATED TO LIVE in covenant relationship with your Heavenly Father. The earthly family is designed to be a place to learn of the love of the Lord through daily life in family relationships. Whatever your role in your family, whether you are a father, mother, brother, sister, son, daughter, grandparent, etc., you have a strategic part in living from the covenant of peace and extending its provisions to your family.

I bless you to continue deepening the love of the Lord in your life in order to love Him with all your heart, soul and strength. May you diligently teach the instruction of the Lord from His Word to your children, whether they are your natural or spiritual children. I pray that these times of teaching have the intended outcome of being fruitful and life giving to your family.

I bless you with the courage, determination, resolve and strength to serve the Lord your God each and every moment of the day. May your steadfast love for the Lord empower others in your family to follow Him as well.

As you fear Him, I bless you to know the everlasting mercy of the Lord on you. May you see His righteousness come to your children's children as you keep His covenant and remember to follow His instructions. I bless you to see the promise in Scripture fulfilled for you that the house of the righteous will stand.

Beloved, I bless you to live from your covenant position as a child of God, which makes you His heir and co-heir with Christ. I bless you with strength to live victoriously in the sufferings with Him in order to be glorified with your Heavenly Father. I bless you in the name of Yeshua, in the name of Jesus.

Chapter 2

COVENANT IN FAMILY #2

"Therefore know that the LORD your God, He is God, the faithful God who keeps covenant and mercy for a thousand generations with those who love Him and keep His commandments."

—DEUTERONOMY 7:9

AS WE CONTINUE WITH PRAYERS OF REPENTANCE for not keeping covenant in our families and replacing them with the truth, nature and character of God that are found in Scripture, may we grow in our relationship with our family. Whether or not families understand or talk about covenant, it is modeled and passed along generationally to the children—families by nature are in a covenant relationship with each other.

Family relationships are meant to reflect and be modeled after the relationship of God the Father with His Son and with Holy Spirit, and the relationship of God to His people. God defines His role with Israel as a father and son relationship. The Lord instructed Moses to say to Pharaoh, "Israel is My son, My firstborn" (Ex 4:22). Thus, the concept that the Lord is our Father originates with Him.

Defilement of covenant in the family misrepresents the covenant relationship of God to our families. As we repent of sin and replace with the goodness of God, may we grow in our understanding of covenant and the ability to live from covenant within the context of our families. May we be blessed in our generations by the Lord and receive His everlasting mercy as we stand in awe of the Lord our God.

REPENTANCE

AS A MEMBER OF THE ROYAL PRIESTHOOD, please repent for not keeping covenant with the Lord by breaking covenant in the family on behalf of yourself, your generations and your nation, and on behalf of your nation for the following:

- not loving your family as yourself (Matt 22:39)
- not forgiving family members and holding bitterness, therefore committing murder in your heart (Matt 5:21-26; Matt 6:15; 1 John 3:15)
  - bitterness is comprised of unforgiveness, resentment, retaliation, anger, hatred, violence and murder
- brother delivering brother to death (Matt 10:21)
- father delivering child to death (Matt 10:21)
- children raising up against parent to put them to death (Matt 10:21)
- having jealousy/envy toward family members (Prov 14:30; Prov 27:4)
- rejecting children (Ps 27:10)
- speaking ill of brother is slandering your mother's son (Ps 50:20)
- judging family members (Matt 7:1-6)

Please repent of the list above on behalf of yourself, your generations and your nation as to how you have hurt others by these actions.

Replacement

As a member of the Royal Priesthood, *please replace with the following:*

- *loving others as you love yourself (Matt 22:39)*
- *forgiving your family members (Matt 6:14)*
- *living in the light in order to combat hatred of family members (1 John 1:7; 1 John 2:9-11)*
- *having love that fights against hatred of family members (1 John 2:9-11)*
- *having a sound heart to war against jealousy/envy of family members (Prov 14:30)*
- *breaking any curses that may have been directed from you toward others in your jealousy of them (Prov 27:4)*
- *having relationship with the Lord and knowing that He will take care of you when your father and mother forsake you (Ps 27:10)*
- *speaking words from your mouth that are pleasing to the Lord (Ps 19:14)*
- *having God's mercy to overcome the judgment of others toward you (James 2:13)*

Forgiveness

I choose to forgive from my heart, (person's name), for how he/she did not keep covenant of the Lord in the family by (fill in from list below), which caused injury to myself and/or my loved ones, either now or in the past.

- not loving you as they love themselves
- holding bitterness toward you, which is comprised of unforgiveness, resentment, retaliation, anger, hatred, violence and murder
- having a brother who may have risen up against you in order to put you to death
- having a father or mother who may have risen up against you in order to put you to death
- having a child who may have risen up against you as a parent in order to put you to death
- being forsaken by your father or mother
- being envious or jealous of you
- speaking ill of you or your children and this being slander
- judging you

BLESS ISRAEL

DEAR HEAVENLY FATHER, I am so thankful that You show us in Scripture what a covenant in family is meant to be through Your faithfulness to Israel and all the Jews. You are a good Father to Israel. I bless Israel to live from the covenant relationship You have with them as their Father. Thank You for being true to Your covenant with Your beloved and chosen people, amen.

STEWARDSHIP & GROWTH IN SPIRITUAL AUTHORITY

DEAR HEAVENLY FATHER, please show me how to live with a greater understanding of covenant within the context of my family.

- What aspects of covenant pertaining to family do I need to learn from You that I do not yet know?

- What do I need to do to begin implementing these aspects of covenant?

- Who do I need to bless in my family from the covenant I have with them?

- How can I bless my family with living from covenantal relationship with them in ways I have not previously done?

- Please show me the timing of when to implement these blessings.

Blessing

Beloved, your Heavenly Father created you to live in covenant relationship with Him in the framework of family. Whether or not your family of origin lived from a life-giving understanding of covenant, your Heavenly Father shows You in His Word and through your relationship with Him how to live from the fullness of the blessings and provisions of covenant in the context of family.

I bless you to live from the covenant relationship as son or daughter of the Most High God. I encourage you to seek His face and to know Him intimately as a good Father who loves you and has good plans for your future (Jer 29:11). As you grow and deepen in the love your Heavenly

Father has for you, I bless your love to grow for your family. May all the things you learn and have revealed to you from the Lord about His covenant with you be foundational to how you live in covenant with your earthly family.

I bless you to know your Heavenly Father will take care of any recompense needed on your behalf (Rom 12:19). From the security that comes from knowing He will take care of all wrong done toward you, I bless you to forgive your family members for any wrongs, either real or perceived, that they have committed against you. I encourage you to release them of any debts caused by their actions or words that have caused you pain.

I bless you to be full of the love and light of the Lord. The light of the Lord is powerful and effective in coming against the bitterness and hatred that stems from unforgiveness. I bless you to walk in the light as the Lord is in the light, in order that you may have fellowship with one another. As you love, you walk in the light of the Lord.

I bless you with a sound heart in order to be strong against the attacks of jealousy and envy that the enemy may bring upon you. I bless you to forgive your family members who may be jealous toward you and seek to destroy the good work the Lord is doing in and through you. May the Lord show you these attacks of jealousy and how you can break any curses that come against you so that you may stand victorious in Him against the wiles of the devil.

If your earthly father and mother have forsaken you, I bless you to know and receive the care of the Lord to love you as Father and mother. I bless you to heal from the mourning and abandonment of your earthly father and mother. If their rejection of you came as a result of their woundedness, or blatant disregard for you, I bless you to see this from another Hebrew definition of "forsake," which means, "to let loose, to set free, let go." I bless you to be set free of their abandonment, actions, anger, bitterness, behavior, rejection, thoughts, or words directed at you. I bless you to be set free from any of their beliefs about you that would keep you from moving into your birthright. I bless you to live from the place of knowing that you are not abandoned, forsaken, or orphaned. I bless you to live as a child of the Most High God. I bless you to know you are loved by your Heavenly Father and are now free to walk in greater expressions of your destiny.

I bless you to know the mercy of the Lord for you that triumphs over the judgments that may have come against you from your family. I bless you to be set free from the condemnation and guilt that comes as a result of another's judgment against you. I bless you to forgive those who have judged you, so you may be forgiven of the judgments you have participated in against others. May you live from the freedom of the mercy and forgiveness the Lord has for you.

Beloved, I bless you to live from the life-giving nature of the covenant the Lord has with you as Father. I bless you with wisdom and knowledge as to how to live in covenant relationship with your family. I bless you in the name of Yeshua, in the name of Jesus.

Chapter 3

COVENANT IN FAMILIES #3

But the mercy of the Lord is from everlasting to everlasting
On those who fear Him,
And His righteousness to children's children,
To such as keep His covenant,
And to those who remember His commandments to do them.
—Psalm 103:17-18

Participation in the occult can be obvious such as outright Satan worship, to seemingly more benign and socially acceptable practices like horoscopes and the Ouija board, to perhaps more hidden methods of participation in witchcraft through means of control. The word "occult" is defined by Webster: "Hidden from the eye or understanding; invisible; secret; unknown; undiscovered; undetected; as the occult qualities of matter. The occult sciences are magic, necromancy, etc." Whether participation in the occult is overt or covert, it is of utmost importance to repent of the sin of the occult and breaking covenant with the Lord that occurs through these practices.

An aspect of the occult included in this chapter is to repent of control, as it is witchcraft. The Word of God is clear that witchcraft is sin (1 Sam 15:23). There does not seem to be a specific reference in the Bible that links control to witchcraft. However, the biblical foundation for this may in fact be that the Lord gives each of us free will to choose what we are to do. Control seeks to take away a person's free will to choose. Clearly, anything in opposition to the way the Lord does something is sin. A very convincing aspect that control is witchcraft comes from the lure in advertising witchcraft from practitioners stating that if a person wants to control someone, they can do so through witchcraft. Control at its basic form is witchcraft. This means that anytime we seek to control someone, we are involved in witchcraft.

Repentance of fear will be included in this section as fear is the underlying means for a person to control others. In addition, fear in a person gives permission to be controlled by another. In order to overcome the evil of control with good, the application of the antidote to controlling others and being controlled is the perfect love of the Lord that casts out fear (1 John 1:18).

The purpose of this chapter is to repent of occult practices in the family. Even though you may not know of any occult activity in your life or your generations, please pray through this area anyway. By its nature, occult means to be hidden and secret. There may be aspects of occult practices in your generations that the enemy has kept hidden from you. By doing so, he gains legal ground. At the completion of this chapter, the Lord may lead you to further work of repentance in this area in your life and that of your family. Please be encouraged to research the many Christian books and resources online for specific topics of breaking free of the occult.

Let us move forward in our journey in deepening our covenant relationship to the Lord by repenting of breaking covenant with Him in our families related to the occult.

Repentance

"You shall have no other gods before Me."
—Exodus 20:3

For rebellion is as the sin of witchcraft,
and stubbornness is as iniquity and idolatry.
—1 Samuel 15:23

As a member of the Royal Priesthood, please repent for not keeping covenant with the Lord on behalf of yourself, your generations and your nation for the following:

- rebellion, witchcraft, stubbornness, iniquity and idolatry (1 Sam 15:23)
- fear that is the root to controlling others
- fear that allows others to control us
- witchcraft and control of others (1 Sam 15:23)
- allowing others to control us or our family members (Titus 1:8)
- participation in the occult (1 Sam 15:23; 2 Tim 3:5)
- secret arts (Ex 7:11 ESV)
- enchantments (Ex 7:11)
- turning to and seeking out mediums (Lev 19:31; Lev 20:6; Is 8:19)
- turning to and seeking out familiar spirits/necromancers—inquiring of the dead on behalf of the living (Lev 19:31; Lev 20:6; Is 8:19)
- being a medium (Lev 19:31; Lev 20:6; Is 8:19)
- being a necromancer (Lev 19:31 ESV; Lev 20:6 ESV; Is 8:19 ESV)
- being a wizard (Lev 19:31)
- astrology, horoscopes (Deut 4:19)
- being a sorcerer (Deut 18:10; Gal 5:20; Rev 21:8)

- interpreting omens (Deut 18:10)
- divination (Deut 18:10 ESV)
- practicing witchcraft (Deut 18:10)
- being a charmer (Deut 18:11 ESV)
- conjuring spells (Deut 18:11)
- being a spiritist (Deut 18:11)
- being one who calls up the dead (Deut 18:11)
- burning child in offering/child sacrifice (2 Ki 21:6 ESV; 2 Chr 33:6 ESV)
- practicing fortune-telling and soothsaying (2 Ki 21:6)
- seeking omens (2 Ki 21:6 ESV; 2 Chr 33:6 ESV)
- consulting spiritists (2 Ki 21:6)
- turning to and seeking out wizards (Is 8:19)
- prophesying lies or false visions in the name of the Lord (Jer 14:14)
- sewing magic charms and making veils for head of persons of every stature to hunt for souls (Ezek 13:18)
- divination of shaking arrows, consulting teraphim/idols and looking at the liver (Ezek 21:21)
- being an enchanter (Dan 2:10 ESV)
- being an astrologer (Dan 2:10)
- having a spirit of divination (Acts 16:16)
- practicing magic arts (Acts 19:19)
- being an idolater (Gal 5:20; Rev 21:8)

Please repent of not keeping covenant with the Lord through worshipping idols or other gods in the family on behalf of yourself, your generations, and your nation for the following:

- transgressing the covenant of the Lord by serving other gods (Josh 23:16)

- being unfaithful to God by playing the adulteress and harlot when worshipping other gods (Ps 106:36-39; Hos 4:12)
- provoking God to jealousy in worship of foreign gods (Deut 32:16)
- provoking God to anger with abominations (Deut 32:16)
- worshipping the gods of Egypt (Ex 12:12)
- worshipping the golden calf (Ex 32:1-35)
  - Israel borrowed this from Egypt
- sacrificing children to Molech (Lev 18:21)
  - Molech means, "king" [H4432]
- worshipping Baal-Peor, god of Moabites (Num 25:3)
  - Baal-Peor means, "lord of the gap" [H1187]
- worshipping the gods of the Amorites (Josh 24:15)
- serving Baal (Judg 2:13)
  - Baal means, "lord" [H1168]
- serving the Ashtoreths, the goddess of the Canaanites (Judg 2:13)
  - Ashtoreth means, "star" [H6252]
  - fertility goddess
- making Baal-Berith a god (Judg 8:33; Judg 9:4)
  - Baal-Berith means, "lord of the covenant" [H1170]
  - god of the Philistines
- serving Asherah (Judg 3:7; 1 Ki 18:19)
  - Asherah means, "groves (for idol worship)" [H842]
  - Asherah is the supposed consort for Baal
- worshipping Dagon (1 Sam 5:2)
  - Dagon means, "a fish" [H1712]
  - deity of fertility
- worshipping Baal-Zebub of Ekron (2 Ki 1:2, 3, 6, 16)
  - Baal-Zebub means, "lord of the fly" [H1176]
  - Beelzebub in Greek [G954] means, "lord of the house" and is a

name of Satan, prince of evil spirits

- ◆ Beelzebub in Greek comes from the Hebrew word [H1176] which means, "lord of the fly"
- ◆ Beelzebub, the ruler of demons (Matt 12:24)
- worshipping Rimmon of Syria (2 Ki 5:18)
  - ◆ Rimmon means, "pomegranate" [H7417]
  - ◆ deity of wind, rain, and storm
- worshipping Succoth Benoth of Babylon (2 Ki 17:30)
  - ◆ Succoth Benoth means, "the daughter's booth" [H5524]
- worshipping Nergal of Cuth (2 Ki 17:30)
  - ◆ Nergal means, "hero" [H5370]
- worshipping Ashima of Hamath in Syria (2 Ki 17:30)
  - ◆ Ashima means, "guiltiness: I will make desolate" [H807]
- worshipping Nibhaz and Tartak of the Avites (2 Ki 17:31)
  - ◆ Nibhaz means, "the barker" [H5026]
  - ◆ Tartak means, "prince of darkness" [H8662]
- burning children in fire to Adrammelech and Anammelech, the gods of Sepharvaim (2 Ki 17:31)
  - ◆ Adrammelech means, "honor of the king" [H152]
  - ◆ Anammelech means, "image of the king" [H6048]
- worshipping Nehushtan, the bronze serpent made by Moses (2 Ki 18:4)
  - ◆ Nehustan means, "a thing of brass" [H5180]
- worshipping the gods of Hamath and Arpad (2 Ki 18:34; Is 36:19)
- worshipping the gods of Sepharvaim (2 Ki 18:34; Is 36:19)
- worshipping the gods of Hena and Ivah (2 Ki 18:34)
- worshipping of Astoreth, the abomination of the Sidonians (2 Ki 23:13)
  - ◆ Astoreth means, "star" [H6253]

- worshipping Chemosh, the abminaton of the Moabites (2 Ki 23:13)
  - ◆ Chemosh means, "subduer" [H3645]
  - ◆ child sacrifices were made to this god
- worshipping Milcom the abomination of the Ammonites (2 Ki 23:13)
  - ◆ Milcom means, "great king" [H4445]
  - ◆ also known as "Molech"
  - ◆ child sacrifices were made to this god
- worshipping gods of Edom (2 Chr 25:20)
- worshipping and sacrificing to the gods of Damascus (2 Chr 28:23)
- worshipping the gods of Syria (2 Chr 28:23)
- worshipping the gods of Babylon (Is 21:9)
- worshipping Bel of the Moabites, Babylonians and Ammonites (Is 46:1; Jer 51:44)
  - ◆ Bel means, "lord" [H1078]
  - ◆ possibly same as Baal
  - ◆ chief Babylonian deity
- worshipping Nebo of the Babylonians (Is 46:1)
  - ◆ Nebo means, "prophet" [H5015]
  - ◆ a Babylonian deity who presided over learning and letters; corresponds to Greek Hermes, Latin Mercury, and Egyptian Thoth
- worshipping Gad (Is 65:11)
  - ◆ Gad means, "fortune, good fortune" [H1409]
- worshipping Meni in Babylon (Is 65:11)
  - ◆ Meni means, "fate" or "fortune" [H4507]
- family participation in worshipping the Queen of Heaven—children, father, mother (Jer 7:18)
- serving and worshipping other gods (Jer 25:6)
- burning incense to Baal (Jer 32:29)

- pouring out drink offerings to other gods (Jer 32:29)
- provoking the Lord to anger through worship of other gods (Jer 32:29)
- worshipping the gods of No in ancient Thebes, Egypt (Jer 46:25)
  - No means, "disrupting" [H4996]
- worshipping the gods of Moab (Jer 48:35)
- offering sacrifices in high places (Jer 48:35)
- burning incense to other gods (Jer 48:35)
- worshipping Merodach of the Babylonians (Jer 50:2)
  - Merodach means, "thy rebellion" [H4781]
  - chief deity in the time of Nebuchadnezzar
- worshipping Tammuz (Ezek 8:14)
  - Tammuz means, "sprout of life" [H8542]
  - Babylonian/Sumerian deity of food or vegetation
- worshipping Chiun of the Babylonians (Amos 5:26)
  - Chiun means, "an image" or "pillar" [H3594]
- swearing by the Lord and Milcom (Zeph 1:5)
  - Milcom is an Ammonite god also called Molech
- worshipping Jupiter or Zeus from Greece (Act 14:12)
  - Jupiter or Zeus means, "a father of helps" [G2203]
  - national god of Greeks
  - corresponds to Roman Jupiter
- worshipping Mercury or Hermes (Acts 14:12)
  - Mercury or Hermes means, "herald of the gods" [G2060]
  - Hermes is a Greek deity
  - Mercury is the corresponding Roman deity
- worshipping Diana of Ephesus, Greece (Acts 19:24, 27-28, 34-35)
  - Diana means, "complete light: flow restrained" [G735]
- worshipping Castor and Pollux (Acts 28:11 KJV)

- ◆ Greek gods, twin sons of Zeus [G1359]
- ◆ protection for sailors

Please repent of the list above on behalf of yourself, your generations and your nation as to how you have hurt others by these actions.

REPLACEMENT

> *However, when He, the Spirit of truth, has come, He will guide you into all truth; for He will not speak on His own authority, but whatever He hears He will speak; and He will tell you things to come.*
> —JOHN 16:13

> *Blessed are those who do His commandments, that they may have the right to the tree of life, and may enter through the gates into the city.*
> —REVELATION 22:14

AS A MEMBER OF THE ROYAL PRIESTHOOD, *please replace what was repented of in the above lists in order to overcome evil with good with the following:*

- *loving the Lord with all your heart, soul and strength (Deut 6:5)*
- *putting away other gods (Josh 24:23)*
- *inclining your heart to the Lord God of Israel (Josh 24:23)*
- *being saved comes by calling on the name of the Lord (Joel 2:32; Acts 2:21; Rom 10:13)*
- *entering into and living from the provision of the covenant of life and peace with the Lord as a member of the Royal Priesthood (Mal 2:4-5; 1 Pet 2:9)*

- *receiving protection from the Lord of Hosts—the Commander-in-Chief of the armies of angels—who makes the covenant of peace/shalom with you (Mal 2:4)*
- *looking to the Spirit of truth for things to come (John 16:13)*
- *being more than a conqueror through Him who loves you (Rom 8:37)*
- *turning away from those who take part in and practice the occult (2 Tim 3:5)*
- *having redemption through the blood of Christ (Eph 1:7)*
- *being forgiven of sins (Eph 1:7)*
- *obtaining your inheritance in Christ (Eph 1:11)*
- *being sealed with the Holy Spirit of promise (Eph 1:13)*
- *putting on the full armor of God (Eph 6:10-18)*
- *being of God as one of His children (1 John 4:4)*
- *overcoming the spirits that do not confess Yeshua/Jesus has come in the flesh (1 John 4:1-5)*
- *living from the truth that greater is He that dwells in you than he who is in the world (1 John 4:4)*
- *receiving the perfect love of the Father to cast out all fear (1 John 4:18)*
- *following the commandments and instructions of the Lord that you may have the right to the tree of life (Rev 22:14)*

FORGIVENESS

I CHOOSE TO FORGIVE FROM MY HEART, (person's name), for how he/she did not keep covenant of the Lord in the family by (fill in from list below), which caused injury to myself and/or my loved ones, either now or in the past.

- committing rebellion, witchcraft, stubbornness, iniquity and idolatry
- using fear that is the root to controlling me
- participating in witchcraft and control directed at me
- allowing others to control me
- participating in the occult
- any other items the Lord leads you to forgive others according to the repentance lists in the above section

BLESS ISRAEL

DEAR HEAVENLY FATHER, thank You for Your everlasting covenant of shalom with Israel (Is 54:10; Ez 37:26). Please pour out Your perfect love in the hearts of all Jews so that they will not fear. May they always and only incline their hearts to You, the Lord God of Israel (Josh 24:23). Please bless and strengthen Your chosen people to have the courage and steadfastness to serve You with all their heart, soul and strength. Thank You for Your faithfulness to Your covenant with Israel. Please give me the wisdom needed to know how to live in agreement with Your covenant of shalom with Israel, amen.

STEWARDSHIP & GROWTH IN SPIRITUAL AUTHORITY

DEAR HEAVENLY FATHER, thank You for Your forgiveness to me in the areas regarding the occult activities in my life and in my generations.

- What areas in my life do I need to change in order to be faithful in covenant with You regarding not being involved in the realm of the occult?

- Are there relationships that I am in that are not healthy for me to maintain that may exert control over me, thereby weakening my self-control?

- If I do need to make changes in this area, what steps do I need to take to make them?

- What resources do I need in order to accomplish this?

- Who do I know that is trustworthy to keep me in prayer during this time of implementation?

- How and when would You like me to pray and intercede for others regarding freedom from the occult?

Blessing

Beloved, you are greatly loved by your Father in Heaven. He made a covenant of peace with Israel, which is available to you through relationship with Yeshua, Jesus Christ. The Hebrew word for "peace" is "shalom" which includes meanings, "safety; soundness in body; welfare; and peace with God, especially in covenant relationship." Shalom comes from a root word that means, "to be in a covenant of peace."

Beloved, hear the Word of the Lord for you.

"For the mountains shall depart
And the hills be removed,
But My kindness shall not depart from you,
Nor shall My covenant of peace be removed,"
Says the LORD, who has mercy on you (Isaiah 54:10).

"There is no peace," says the LORD, "for the wicked" (Isaiah 48:22).

I bless you to live from the understanding that you have a covenant of peace with God. Covenants include protection from enemies. When you became a child of the Most High God, you transfer from the kingdom of darkness to the Kingdom of God. In this transfer of kingdoms, any attack against you from the kingdom of darkness is now an attack against the Kingdom of God. The Lord will fight for you because He has made a covenant of peace with you.

In Malachi, the Lord declares that He as the Lord of Hosts makes the covenant of life and peace (Mal 2:4-5). It is interesting and important to see the connection that the Lord of Hosts makes the covenant of life and peace. The title of God, the Lord of Hosts, describes His role as commander-in-chief over the armies of angels. Along with the fact He makes this covenant, He has the power and might to enforce it. The Lord of Hosts implements the safety and welfare in the covenant of life and peace.

I bless you with the protection that is yours in the covenant of life and peace that is essential when coming out of the occult. I bless you with covenant protection when breaking free from control or witchcraft. I bless you with the protection from the Lord of Hosts as you break free of control and witchcraft that you or your generations have participated in. I bless you with protection while securing your victory as you break free of control and witchcraft directed at you.

Beloved, I bless you to live from the reality of the covenant of life and peace enforced by the Lord of Hosts to keep you safe from attacks from the enemy relating to control, the occult or witchcraft. I bless you to know the Father as the Lord of Hosts. I bless you to know Him as the keeper of the covenant. I bless you to understand in your heart of hearts that you are precious to Him. It pleases Him to keep His promises to you. I bless you to live from the Father's covenant of life and peace that provides for you to live in safety and welfare. I bless you in the name of Yeshua, in the name of Jesus.

PART 2

GOD YOUR FATHER

Is He not your Father, who bought you?
Has He not made you and established you?
—DEUTERONOMY 32:6b

In order to understand how to live in covenant relationship with members of our natural families, we first need to make right our relationship with our Heavenly Father. Therefore, we turn our attention to living in covenant in our relationship with our Heavenly Father. We cannot be in right relationship with our families if we are not living in covenant with our Heavenly Father. Please join together as members of the Royal Priesthood in praying for repentance and replacement concerning our covenant relationship with our Heavenly Father.

Chapter 4

GOD YOUR FATHER #1

Is He not your Father, who bought you?
Has He not made you and established you?
—DEUTERONOMY 32:6b

REPENTANCE & REPLACEMENT

AS A MEMBER OF THE ROYAL PRIESTHOOD, please repent of breaking covenant with your Heavenly Father on behalf of yourself, your generations and your nation for the following and *replace with statements in italics:*

- corrupting yourself (Deut 32:5)
- not being the children of the Lord (Deut 32:5)
- being a perverse and crooked generation (Deut 32:5)
- dealing with the Lord in being foolish and unwise (Deut 32:6)
  - *knowing and living from the truth your Father bought you (Deut 32:6)*
  - *living from the truth your Father made you (Deut 32:6)*
  - *living from the truth that your Father established you (Deut 32:6)*

- being unmindful of the Rock who begot you (Deut 32:18)
- forgetting the God who fathered you (Deut 32:18)

- ◆ *keeping in mind the Rock who made you (Deut 32:18)*
- ◆ *remembering God who fathered you (Deut 32:18)*

- not honoring the Father (Mal 1:6)
- not reverencing Him as Lord and Master (Mal 1:6)
  - ◆ *honoring the Father (Mal 1:6)*
  - ◆ *reverencing Him as Lord and Master (Mal 1:6)*
  - ◆ *the Hebrew word [H113] translated as "master" includes meanings, "lord, master, the Lord God, Lord of the whole earth"*

- not letting your light shine before men (Matt 5:16)
- not allowing others to see your good works either by hiding them and/or not doing them (Matt 5:16)
- not glorifying your Father in Heaven with your light and good works (Matt 5:16)
  - ◆ *letting your light shine before men (Matt 5:16)*
  - ◆ *doing good works and allowing others to see them (Matt 5:16)*
  - ◆ *glorifying your Father in Heaven with your light and good works (Matt 5:16)*

- hating your enemies (Matt 5:43-45)
- cursing those who curse you (Matt 5:43-45)
- not being a true son or daughter to your Heavenly Father by hating your enemies and cursing those who curse you (Matt 5:43-45)
- not being perfect as your Heavenly Father is perfect (Matt 5:45)
  - ◆ *loving your enemies (Matt 5:43-45)*
  - ◆ *blessing those who curse you (Matt 5:43-45)*
  - ◆ *doing good to those who hate you (Matt 5:43-45)*
  - ◆ *praying for those who spitefully use you and persecute you (Matt 5:43-45)*

- *doing these actions as a son or daughter of your Heavenly Father (Matt 5:43-45)*
- *being perfect as your Heavenly Father is perfect (Matt 5:48)*
- *putting on love, which is the bond of perfection (Col 3:14)*
- *having love made perfect in you (1 John 2:5, 4:12, 4:17-18)*

- doing charitable deeds before men to be seen by them in order to have glory from men (Matt 6:1-2)
  - *doing charitable deeds in secret in order to be rewarded by your Heavenly Father (Matt 6:4)*

- praying in order to be seen by men (Matt 6:5)
  - *praying in the secret place in order to be rewarded by your Heavenly Father (Matt 6:6)*

- praying in vain repetitions like the heathen (Matt 6:7)
- not praying in the manner of the Lord's prayer (Matt 6:9-15)
  - *not praying in vain repetitions like the heathen (Matt 6:7)*
  - *praying knowing your Heavenly Father knows what you need before you ask (Matt 6:8)*
  - *praying in the manner of the Lord's prayer (Matt 6:9-15)*
  - *going boldly before the throne of grace to obtain mercy and find grace in time of need (Heb 4:16)*

- not forgiving others their trespasses; therefore, not being forgiven from your Father for your trespasses (Matt 6:15)
  - *forgiving others their trespasses, so your Father will forgive you of your trespasses (Matt 6:14)*

Please repent of the list above on behalf of yourself, your generations and your nation as to how you have hurt the Lord or others by these actions.

Forgiveness

I choose to forgive from my heart, (person's name), for how he/she did not keep covenant of the Lord as Father by (fill in from list below), which caused injury to myself and/or my loved ones, either now or in the past.

- corrupting himself/herself
- not being a child of the Lord
- being of a perverse and crooked generation
- dealing with the Lord in being foolish and unwise
- being unmindful of the Rock who begot him/her
- forgetting the God who fathered him/her
- not honoring the Father
- not reverencing Him as Lord and Master
- not letting his/her light shine before men
- not allowing others to see his/her good works either by hiding them and/or not doing them
- not glorifying his/her Father in Heaven with his/her light and good works
- hating his/her enemies
- cursing those who curse him/her
- not being a true son/daughter to his/her Heavenly Father by hating his/her enemies and cursing those who curse him/her
- not being perfect as his/her Heavenly Father is perfect
- doing charitable deeds before men to be seen by them in order to have glory from men
- praying in order to be seen by men
- praying in vain repetitions like the heathen

- not praying in the manner of the Lord's prayer
- not forgiving others their trespasses; therefore, not being forgiven from the Father for his/her trespasses

Bless Israel

Dear Heavenly Father, thank You for being a Father to Israel and the Jews. I bless them to know and live from the truth that You, as their Father, bought them and made them. I bless all Jews to know that You, as their Father, established them. You have provided everything they need in the covenant of peace You made with Your people. I pray that the Jewish people will be continually mindful of the Rock who begot them and remember who fathered them, amen.

Stewardship & Growth in Spiritual Authority

Dear Heavenly Father, thank You for being my Father. I turn my face to seek You and to grow in intimacy with You.

- What aspects of the crooked and perverse generation in which I live do I participate in that I need to let go of in my life? Please show me these things to let go of as I may be blinded to that which is common around me.
- In what ways am I foolish and unwise in my interactions with and understanding of You?

- What do I need to remove in order to be wise in my interactions with and understanding of You?

- What do I need to add in order to be wise in my interactions with and understanding of You?

- How am I to glorify You as my Father in Heaven with my light and good works?

Please take time to ask your Father anything else that stands out regarding any of the repentance or replacement items listed in the above section.

BLESSING

Beloved, as a member of the Royal Priesthood and dearly loved child of God the Father, I bless you to grow in your relationship with Him as your Father. Understanding how to live in covenant relationship with your Heavenly Father is the basis of learning covenant relationship in the family.

I bless you to know that He is your Father and He bought you. I bless you to know that He established you. Your Father has purposed and secured everything you need to live in covenant relationship with Him. I bless you to live from being established by the Father and to live in the fullness of the covenant He made with you. May you cry to the Lord, "You are my Father, My God, and the rock of my salvation" (Ps 89:26).

Since He is your Heavenly Father and He loves you, I bless you to take heed when He brings correction (2 Sam 7:14). I bless you to know the mercy that your Heavenly Father has toward you (1 Chr 17:13). I bless you to know Him as the Everlasting Father, who is your Redeemer (Is 9:6; Is 63:16). May you always honor your Heavenly Father and give reverence to Him as Lord and Master, the Lord of the Whole Earth (Mal 1:6).

I bless you to let your light shine before men so they may glorify your Father in Heaven. May your good works also give glory to your Heavenly Father.

I bless you to bless those who curse you in order that you may be a son or daughter of your Father in Heaven. I bless you to put on love, which is the bond of perfection, in order to bless those who bless you.

I encourage you to grow in perfect love that you may be perfect as your Father in Heaven is perfect. May His perfect love cast out all fear in order to be made perfect in love.

May you also be perfected in love in order to forgive those who sin against you that you may be forgiven by your Heavenly Father.

I bless you to have a strong identity in the Lord that you seek to please Him and not man. May all your charitable deeds be done in secret so your Heavenly Father can reward you openly.

Beloved, I bless you to have a strong prayer life where you can pray secretly to the Lord in humility. May you approach Him in prayer with thanksgiving, boldness and confidence in order to not pray in vain repetitions. I encourage you to pray according to how Yeshua taught regarding prayer. Your Father knows what you need even before you ask Him. I bless you to grow in your relationship with your Heavenly Father in the name of Yeshua, in the name of Jesus.

Chapter 5

GOD YOUR FATHER #2

[Then He said to His disciples] "Do not fear, little flock, for it is your Father's good pleasure to give you the kingdom."
—LUKE 12:32

REPENTANCE & REPLACEMENT

AS A MEMBER OF THE ROYAL PRIESTHOOD, please repent of breaking covenant with the Lord by not being in right relationship with your Heavenly Father on behalf of yourself, your generations and your nation for the following and *replace with statements in italics:*

- trying to enter the Kingdom of Heaven by saying, "Lord, Lord," but not by obeying Him (Matt 7:21)
  - *obeying and doing the will of your Heavenly Father in order to enter the Kingdom of Heaven (Matt 7:21)*

- not confessing Yeshua/Jesus as Lord before men; therefore, breaking down your relationship with Yeshua/Jesus and the Father (Matt 10:32)
- denying Yeshua/Jesus as Lord before men; therefore, being denied by Yeshua/Jesus before the Father (Matt 10:33)

- *confessing Yeshua/Jesus as Lord before men so Yeshua/Jesus will confess you before the Father (Matt 10:32)*

- not doing the will of your Heavenly Father breaks down your family relationship with the Father and the Son (Matt 12:50)
  - *doing the will of our Heavenly Father and being in right relationship with the Father and Son (Matt 12:50)*

- not making disciples of all the nations (Matt 28:19)
- not baptizing the nations in the name of the Father, Son and Holy Spirit (Matt 28:19)
- not teaching the nations to observe all things the Lord has commanded (Matt 28:20)
  - *making disciples of all the nations (Matt 28:19)*
  - *baptizing the nations in the name of the Father, Son and Holy Spirit (Matt 28:19)*
  - *teaching the nations to observe all things the Lord has commanded (Matt 28:20)*

- having fear (Luke 12:32)
- not believing it is the Father's good pleasure to give you the Kingdom of Heaven (Luke 12:32)
  - *having the perfect love of the Father that casts out fear (1 John 4:18)*
  - *believing and living from the reality that it's the Father's good pleasure to give you the Kingdom of Heaven (Luke 12:32)*

- not being merciful (Luke 6:36)
- not representing your Heavenly Father as merciful when being judgmental (Mic 6:8; Luke 6:36)
  - *being merciful like your Heavenly Father (Luke 6:36)*

- ◆ *doing good by loving mercy (Mic 6:8)*

- doing what you think you ought to do without seeing what the Father is doing (John 5:19)
  - ◆ *following the example of Yeshua/Jesus and only doing what you see the Father doing (John 5:19)*

- thinking that you come to the Lord of your own volition (John 6:65)
  - ◆ *knowing and accepting that it is granted to you by your Father to approach the Messiah (John 6:65)*

- claiming to love the Father but not loving Yeshua/Jesus (John 8:42)
  - ◆ *loving the Father and loving His Son (John 8:42)*

- not serving or following Yeshua/Jesus; thereby, not being honored by the Father (John 12:26)
  - ◆ *serving and following Yeshua/Jesus so that you can be honored by the Father (John 12:26)*

- not believing and living from the truth that Yeshua/Jesus is the way (John 14:6)
- not believing and living from the truth that Yeshua/Jesus is the truth (John 14:6)
- not believing and living from the truth that Yeshua/Jesus is the life (John 14:6)
  - ◆ *believing and living from the truth that Yeshua/Jesus is the way (John 14:6)*
  - ◆ *believing and living from the truth that Yeshua/Jesus is the truth (John 14:6)*
  - ◆ *believing and living from the truth that Yeshua/Jesus is the life (John 14:6)*

- not believing that Yeshua/Jesus is in the Father and that the Father is in Yeshua/Jesus (John 14:11)
- not believing Yeshua/Jesus based on the sake of the works He performed (John 14:11)
  - *believing Yeshua/Jesus is in the Father and that the Father is in Yeshua/Jesus (John 14:11)*
  - *believing Yeshua/Jesus based on the sake of the works He performed (John 14:11)*

- not believing in Yeshua/Jesus (John 14:12)
- not believing that you can do the works Yeshua/Jesus performed (John 14:12)
- not doing the works Yeshua/Jesus performed (John 14:12)
- not believing you can do greater works than Yeshua/Jesus since He has gone to the Father (John 14:12)
- not doing greater works than Yeshua/Jesus did now that He has gone to the Father (John 14:12)
  - *believing in Yeshua/Jesus (John 14:12)*
  - *believing you can do the works Yeshua/Jesus performed (John 14:12)*
  - *doing the works Yeshua/Jesus performed (John 14:12)*
  - *believing you can do greater works than Yeshua/Jesus did since He has gone to the Father (John 14:12)*
  - *doing greater works than Yeshua/Jesus did now that He has gone to the Father (John 14:12)*

Please repent of the list above on behalf of yourself, your generations and your nation as to how you have hurt your Heavenly Father and others by these actions.

FORGIVENESS

I CHOOSE TO FORGIVE FROM MY HEART, (person's name), for how he/she did not keep covenant of the Lord as Father by (fill in from list below), which caused injury to myself and/or my loved ones, either now or in the past.

- trying to enter the Kingdom of Heaven by saying, "Lord, Lord," but not by obeying Him
- not confessing Yeshua/Jesus as Lord before men; therefore, breaking down his/her relationship with Yeshua/Jesus and the Father
- denying Yeshua/Jesus as Lord before men
- not doing the will of his/her Heavenly Father
- not making disciples of all the nations
- not baptizing the nations in the name of the Father, Son and Holy Spirit
- not teaching the nations to observe all things the Lord has commanded
- having fear
- not believing it is the Father's good pleasure to give him/her the Kingdom of Heaven
- not being merciful
- not representing his/her Father when being judgmental
- doing what he/she thinks he/she ought to do without seeing what the Father is doing
- thinking that he/she comes to the Lord of his/her own volition
- claiming to love the Father but not loving Yeshua/Jesus
- not serving or following Yeshua/Jesus
- not believing and living from the truth that Yeshua/Jesus is the way

- not believing and living from the truth that Yeshua/Jesus is the truth
- not believing and living from the truth that Yeshua/Jesus is the life
- not believing that Yeshua/Jesus is in the Father and that the Father is in Yeshua/Jesus
- not believing Yeshua/Jesus based on the sake of the works He performed
- not believing in Yeshua/Jesus
- not believing that he/she can do the works Yeshua/Jesus performed
- not doing the works Yeshua/Jesus performed
- not believing he/she can do greater works than Jesus since He has gone to the Father
- not doing greater works than Yeshua/Jesus did now that He has gone to the Father

Bless Israel

Dear Heavenly Father, on behalf of the members of the Royal Priesthood, I repent for how we have misrepresented Yeshua/Jesus to Israel and the Jews. Please forgive us of not living from the truth that we have one Father and that one God created us. Please forgive us of dealing treacherously with Your people (Mal 2:10). We have profaned the covenant of life and peace that You as the Lord of Hosts made with us as the Royal Priesthood (Mal 2:4-5, 10; Heb 13:8; 1 Pet 2:9). Please grant us mercy. May we please have the opportunity to reconcile with our Jewish brothers and sisters and live with them in covenant as You intended, amen.

STEWARDSHIP & GROWTH
IN SPIRITUAL AUTHORITY

DEAR HEAVENLY FATHER, I turn toward You and seek Your face. As my Father in Heaven, I desire to grow in covenant relationship with You by asking the following questions:

- Are there areas in my life where I say, "Lord, Lord," desiring that to be enough to enter the Kingdom in order to mask over my disobedience?

- Do I truly believe and live from the truth that it is Your good pleasure to give me the Kingdom?

- If not, why do I not believe this?

- Is there something in me that needs healing in order to live from the truth that it is Your good pleasure to give me the Kingdom?

- What do I need to remove from my life in order to live from the truth that it is Your good pleasure to give me the Kingdom?

- What do I need to add in my life so that I may live from the truth that it is Your good pleasure to give me the Kingdom?

- What practical steps do I need to take in order to move into living from the truth that it is Your good pleasure to give me the Kingdom?

The purpose of being given the Kingdom is to be a good steward in building it. Please prepare me for all I need in order to do Your work. I ask this in the name of Yeshua, in the name of Jesus, amen.

Blessing

Beloved, as a member of the Royal Priesthood, you are in a position of family to God the Father, God the Son and God the Holy Spirit. I bless you to grow in your covenant relationship to your Heavenly Father. I encourage you to learn from your Heavenly Father how to live from the provisions of covenant that He has for you. May you learn all that He has for you. May you grow and prosper in the ways of bringing the Kingdom of Heaven to earth.

I bless you to obey and to do the will of your Heavenly Father in order for you to enter the Kingdom of Heaven.

I bless you to confess Yeshua/Jesus as Lord before men. In doing so, Yeshua/Jesus will confess you before the Father. I bless your relationship with the Son to be strong in order for your relationship with your Heavenly Father to grow and be strong as well.

I bless you to know the blessing of covenant relationship that occurs when you do the will of your Heavenly Father. I bless you to live with having a family relationship with the Father, Son and Holy Spirit, as well as having a family relationship to those who do the will of the Father.

I bless you with the wisdom, courage, strength and resources to make disciples of the nations, baptizing them in the name of the Father, Son and Holy Spirit. I bless you to teach the nations to observe all the things the Lord has commanded.

I bless you to know the perfect love of the Father that casts out all fear in your life. I bless you to live in perfect love knowing that it is your

Heavenly Father's good pleasure to give you the Kingdom. May your Heavenly Father show you what it is to live from the Kingdom and from His good pleasure.

I bless you to grow in your ability to be merciful. I bless you to be merciful, just as your Heavenly Father is merciful. I bless you to do good by being merciful.

I bless you to follow the example of Jesus and only do what you see your Heavenly Father doing.

I bless you to remain humble, remembering always that it is your Heavenly Father who grants that you are able to come unto Yeshua/Jesus.

May you continue to grow in your love for both your Heavenly Father and for His Son, Yeshua/Jesus. Being in covenant with your Heavenly Father is contingent upon loving His Son.

I bless you to serve and follow Yeshua HaMashiach, Jesus Christ, in order that you may be honored by your Heavenly Father.

May you live from the fullness of the reality that Yeshua/Jesus is the way, the truth and the life; and that He is the only way to the Heavenly Father. I encourage you to remove anything in your life that takes your feet off the path of the way of Yeshua/Jesus, turns you from the truth, and keeps you from the fullness of His life for you in order that you may walk in the way, the truth and the life made available through Yeshua/Jesus.

I bless you to believe and live from the unity that comes from Yeshua/Jesus being in the Father and that the Father is in Yeshua/Jesus. I bless you to believe Yeshua/Jesus based on the sake of the works He performed.

May you be blessed to do works greater than Yeshua/Jesus did while He was here on earth.

Beloved, I bless you to grow in covenant relationship with your Heavenly Father through the revelation of and in relationship with Yeshua HaMashiach, Jesus Christ. I bless you in the name of Yeshua, in the name of Jesus.

Chapter 6

GOD YOUR FATHER #3

For you did not receive the spirit of bondage again to fear, but you received the Spirit of adoption by whom we cry out, "Abba, Father."
—ROMANS 8:15

REPENTANCE & REPLACEMENT

As a member of the Royal Priesthood, please repent of not keeping covenant with the Lord by not being in right relationship with your Heavenly Father on behalf of yourself, your generations and your nation for the following and *replace with statements in italics:*

- not keeping covenant with your Heavenly Father by not keeping the commandments of Yeshua HaMashiach, Jesus Christ (John 14:23)
- not keeping covenant with your Heavenly Father by not truly loving Yeshua/Jesus by not obeying Him (John 14:23)
    - *keeping covenant with your Heavenly Father by keeping the commandments of the Yeshua HaMashiach, Christ Jesus (John 14:23)*
    - *keeping covenant with your Heavenly Father by loving Yeshua/Jesus by obeying Him and keeping His commandments (John 14:23)*

- *keeping covenant with your Heavenly Father by loving Yeshua/Jesus results in being loved by the Father (John 14:23)*
- *keeping covenant with your Heavenly Father by loving Yeshua/Jesus results in being loved by Yeshua/Jesus and having Him manifest Himself to you who love Him (John 14:23)*

- not keeping covenant with your Heavenly Father by not keeping the word of Yeshua HaMashiach/Jesus Christ, which is the word of the Father (John 14:24)
  - *keeping covenant with your Heavenly Father by keeping the word of Yeshua HaMashiach/Jesus Christ and keeping the word of the Father (John 14:24)*
  - *keeping covenant with your Heavenly Father by means of relationship with both the Father and Son, who make Their home with those who love Them and keep Their words (John 14:24)*

- not keeping covenant with your Heavenly Father by not following Yeshua's/Jesus' example of keeping the Father's commandments and abiding in His love (John 15:10)
  - *keeping covenant with your Heavenly Father by keeping the commandments of Yeshua/Jesus as He kept the Father's commandments (John 15:10)*
  - *keeping covenant with your Heavenly Father by abiding in the love of Yeshua/Jesus (John 15:10)*

- not keeping covenant with your Heavenly Father by not being a faithful steward of the things Yeshua/Jesus made known to you that He heard from the Father (John 15:15)
  - *keeping covenant with your Heavenly Father by being true friends of Yeshua/Jesus and being good stewards of the things He made known that which He heard from the Father (John 15:15)*

- not keeping covenant with your Heavenly Father by being prideful and thinking that you chose Yeshua/Jesus (John 15:16)
- not keeping covenant with your Heavenly Father by not asking the Father for things in the name of Yeshua/Jesus in humility and with the understanding of covenant relationship (John 15:16; John 16:13-15)
  - *keeping covenant with your Heavenly Father by asking the Father for things in the name of Yeshua/Jesus in humility and with the understanding of covenant relationship (John 15:16; John 16:13-15)*

- not keeping covenant with your Heavenly Father by hating Yeshua/Jesus (John 15:23)
  - *keeping covenant with your Heavenly Father by loving Yeshua/Jesus (John 16:27)*
  - *keeping covenant with your Heavenly Father by believing Yeshua/Jesus came from God (John 16:27)*

- not keeping covenant with your Heavenly Father by not being one with the Father and with Yeshua/Jesus (John 17:21)
  - *keeping covenant with your Heavenly Father and Yeshua/Jesus by being one in them (John 17:21)*

- not keeping covenant with your Heavenly Father by not knowing Him (John 17:25)
  - *keeping covenant with your Heavenly Father by knowing Him (John 17:25)*

- not keeping covenant with your Heavenly Father by not living from the truth of the Spirit of adoption you have received (Rom 8:15)

> ◆ *keeping covenant with your Heavenly Father by living from the Spirit of adoption and crying out, "Abba, Father" (Rom 8:15)*

- not keeping covenant with your Heavenly Father by not glorifying the God and Father of Yeshua HaMashiach, the Lord Jesus Christ, with the saints with one mind and mouth (Rom 15:6)
  - ◆ *keeping covenant with your Heavenly Father by glorifying the God and Father of Yeshua HaMashiach, the Lord Jesus Christ, with the saints with one mind and mouth (Rom 15:6)*

Please repent of the list above on behalf of yourself, your generations and your nation as to how you have hurt your Heavenly Father or others by these actions.

FORGIVENESS

I CHOOSE TO FORGIVE FROM MY HEART, (person's name), for how he/she did not keep covenant of the Lord as Father by (fill in from list below), which caused injury to myself and/or my loved ones, either now or in the past.

- not keeping covenant with his/her Heavenly Father by not having and not keeping the commandments of Yeshua HaMashiach, Jesus Christ
- not keeping covenant with his/her Heavenly Father by not truly loving Yeshua/Jesus by not obeying Him
- not keeping covenant with his/her Heavenly Father by not keeping the word of Yeshua HaMashiach, Jesus Christ, which is the word of the Father

- not keeping covenant with his/her Heavenly Father by not following Yeshua's/Jesus' example of keeping the Father's commandments and abiding in His love
- not keeping covenant with his/her Heavenly Father by not being a faithful steward of the things Yeshua/Jesus made known to him/her that He heard from the Father
- not keeping covenant with his/her Heavenly Father by being prideful and thinking that he/she chose Yeshua/Jesus
- not keeping covenant with his/her Heavenly Father by not asking the Father for things in the name of Yeshua/Jesus in humility and with the understanding of covenant relationship
- not keeping covenant with his/her Heavenly Father by hating Yeshua/Jesus
- not keeping covenant with his/her Heavenly Father by not being one with the Father and with Yeshua/Jesus
- not keeping covenant with his/her Heavenly Father by not knowing Him
- not keeping covenant with his/her Heavenly Father by not living from the truth of the Spirit of adoption he/she has received
- not keeping covenant with his/her Heavenly Father by not glorifying the God and Father of Yeshua HaMashiach, the Lord Jesus Christ, with the saints with one mind and mouth

Bless Israel

Dear Heavenly Father, thank You for loving Israel and the Jews as their Father. Please give them strength as Your sons and daughters in order to walk in Your ways. I bless Your people to grow in their love for

You. May they continue to embrace You as their Father. For the Jews who do not know You as Father, please draw their hearts to You with Your love for them, amen.

Stewardship & Growth
in Spiritual Authority

Dear Heavenly Father, I turn toward You and seek Your face. As my Father in heaven, I desire to grow in covenant relationship with You by asking the following questions:

- Are there areas in my life where I have broken covenant with You by not being a faithful steward of the things Yeshua/Jesus made known to me that He heard from You?

- What do I need to remove from my life that keeps me from faithfully stewarding these things that Yeshua/Jesus made known to me in His word that came from You?

- What do I need to add into my life that I may faithfully steward these things that Yeshua/Jesus made known to me in His word that came from You?

- Are there areas in my life where I break covenant with You, my Father, by not living from the truth of the Spirit of adoption that I have received from You?

- What needs to be healed in my life that I may keep covenant with You as My Father as I live from the truth of the Spirit of adoption that I have received from You?

- What steps do I need to take to prepare myself to receive the healing from You?

BLESSING

BELOVED, AS A MEMBER OF THE ROYAL PRIESTHOOD and a child of your Father in Heaven, I bless you to grow in your understanding of how to live in covenant with the Father through Yeshua/Jesus.

I bless you to keep covenant with your Heavenly Father by having and keeping the commandments of the Yeshua HaMashiach, Christ Jesus. May you be strengthened in covenant with your Heavenly Father as you obey and keep the commandments of Yeshua/Jesus.

May you know the blessings of being loved by your Heavenly Father that come as a result of loving Yeshua/Jesus. It is in loving Yeshua/Jesus that results in being loved by Him and having Yeshua/Jesus manifest Himself to those who love Him.

I encourage you to remain in covenant with your Heavenly Father by keeping the word of Yeshua HaMashiach, Jesus Christ, and keeping the word of the Father.

May you keep covenant with your Heavenly Father by means of relationship with both the Father and Son, who make Their home with those who love Them and keep Their words.

I encourage you to remain in covenant with your Heavenly Father by keeping the commandments of Yeshua/Jesus as He kept the Father's commandments. May you always keep covenant with your Heavenly Father by abiding in the love of Yeshua/Jesus.

I bless you to keep covenant with your Heavenly Father by being true friends of Yeshua/Jesus and being good stewards of the things He made known that He heard from the Father.

I encourage you to keep covenant with your Heavenly Father by asking the Father for things in the name of Yeshua/Jesus in humility and from the understanding of covenant relationship.

May you always keep covenant with your Heavenly Father by loving Yeshua/Jesus. I bless you to keep covenant with your Heavenly Father by believing Yeshua/Jesus came from God.

Child of the Most High God, I bless you to keep covenant with your Heavenly Father and Yeshua/Jesus by being one in Them. May you always keep covenant with your Heavenly Father by knowing Him.

I bless you to keep covenant with your Heavenly Father by living from the Spirit of adoption and crying out, "Abba, Father."

Beloved, may you always keep covenant with your Heavenly Father by glorifying the God and Father of Yeshua HaMashiach, the Lord Jesus Christ, with the saints with one mind and mouth. I bless you in the name of Yeshua, in the name of Jesus.

Chapter 7

GOD YOUR FATHER #4

*Giving thanks to the Father who has qualified us to
be partakers of the inheritance of the saints in the light.*

—COLOSSIANS 1:12

REPENTANCE & REPLACEMENT

AS A MEMBER OF THE ROYAL PRIESTHOOD, please repent of not keeping covenant with the Lord by not being in right relationship with your Heavenly Father on behalf of yourself, your generations and your nation for the following and *replace with statements in italics:*

- not keeping covenant with your Heavenly Father by not believing in one Father and believing there are many gods (1 Cor 8:5)
  - *keeping covenant with your Heavenly Father by believing and declaring there is one God, the Father (1 Cor 8:6)*
  - *knowing you were created for Him (1 Cor 8:6)*
  - *believing there is one Yeshua HaMashiach, the Lord Jesus Christ (1 Cor 8:6)*
  - *knowing it is through Him that you live (1 Cor 8:6)*

- not keeping covenant by believing that God and Father of Yeshua HaMashiach, the Lord Jesus Christ, is harsh and without mercy (2

Cor 1:3)

- not keeping covenant by not believing He is the Father of mercies (2 Cor 1:3)
    - *living in covenant with the Father by believing He is the Father of mercies (2 Cor 1:3)*

- not keeping covenant by not believing that God and the Father of Yeshua HaMashiach, the Lord Jesus Christ, is the God of all comfort when you are in tribulation (2 Cor 1:4)
    - *living in covenant with your Father by believing and living from the reality that He is the God of all comfort, who comforts you when you are in tribulation (2 Cor 1:4)*
    - *living in covenant with your Father and receiving His comfort so you may in turn comfort others when they are in trouble (2 Cor 1:4)*

- not living from or receiving the covenant provisions of grace and peace that comes from God the Father and Yeshua HaMashiach, the Lord Jesus Christ (Gal 1:3)
    - *living in covenant relationship according to the will of God and Father, that you may be delivered from the evil of this age by Yeshua HaMashiach, the Lord Jesus Christ, who gave Himself for your sins (Gal 1:4)*

- not keeping covenant—or not receiving the blessings of covenant—by not living from, denying or not believing the truth that the God and Father of Yeshua HaMashiach, the Lord Jesus Christ, has blessed you with every spiritual blessing in the heavenly places in Yeshua/Jesus (Eph 1:3)
    - *living from the covenantal blessings that the God and Father of*

Yeshua HaMashiach, the Lord Jesus Christ, has blessed you by giving you every spiritual blessing in the heavenly places in Christ (Eph 1:3)

- not living in covenant by not believing the Father of glory gives you the spirit of wisdom and revelation in the knowledge of Him (Eph 1:17)
  - *living in covenant and believing the Father of glory gives you the spirit of wisdom and revelation in the knowledge of Him (Eph 1:17)*

- not living in covenant by not receiving all that the Father of glory wants to give you concerning the spirit of wisdom and revelation in the knowledge of Him (Eph 1:17)
  - *living in covenant with the Father of glory and receiving from Him all He desires to give you through the spirit of wisdom and revelation in the knowledge of Him (Eph 1:17)*

- not keeping covenant by not believing that through Yeshua HaMashiach, Jesus Christ, you have access by one Holy Spirit to God the Father (Eph 2:18)
  - *living in covenant relationship through Yeshua HaMashiach, Jesus Christ, and accessing the Father through the Holy Spirit (Eph 2:18)*

- not living in covenant with your Father by not acknowledging the role of the Holy Spirit who gives you access to Him (Eph 2:18)
  - *living in covenant with your Father by acknowledging the role of the Holy Spirit who give access to Him (Eph 2:18)*

- not living in covenant with the Father by choosing of your own accord not to bend the knee to Yeshua/Jesus and confessing with your tongue that He is Lord to the glory of God the Father (Phil 2:10-11)

- ♦ *living in covenant relationship with Yeshua HaMashiach, the Lord Jesus Christ, by bending your knees to worship Him and confessing with your tongue that Yeshua HaMashiach, Jesus Christ, is Lord in order to bring glory to God the Father (Phil 2:10-11)*

- not keeping covenant by not giving thanks to the Father and/or not acknowledging that it is He who has qualified you to partake of the inheritance of the saints in the light (Col 1:12)
  - ♦ *keeping covenant with and giving thanks to the Father for qualifying you to partake of the inheritance of the saints in the light (Col 1:12)*

- not keeping covenant by not receiving and partaking of the inheritance of the saints in the light for which the Father qualifies you (Col 1:12)
  - ♦ *keeping covenant with the Father by partaking of the inheritance of the saints in the light for which He qualifies you (Col 1:12)*

- not living in covenant with the Father by not being knit together in love with others in the body of Christ (Col 2:2)
  - ♦ *living in covenant with the Father by being knit together in love with others in the body of Christ (Col 2:2)*

- not attaining in covenant all the riches of the full assurance of understanding the knowledge of the mystery of God the Father (Col 2:2)
  - ♦ *living from the covenant blessings from God of all the riches of the full assurance of understanding the knowledge of the mystery of God the Father (Col 2:2)*

- not living from the covenant blessings of the Father and Christ in whom all treasures of wisdom and knowledge are hidden (Col 2:3)
  - *living from covenant blessings revealed from the Father and Christ, in whom are hidden all treasures of wisdom and knowledge (Col 2:3)*

Please repent of the list above on behalf of yourself, your generations and your nation as to how you have hurt your Heavenly Father or others by these actions.

FORGIVENESS

I CHOOSE TO FORGIVE FROM MY HEART, (person's name), for how he/she did not keep covenant with the Lord as Father by (fill in from list below), which caused injury to myself and/or my loved ones, either now or in the past.

- not keeping covenant with the Father by not believing in one Father and believing there are many gods
- not keeping covenant by believing that God and Father of Yeshua HaMashiach, the Lord Jesus Christ, is harsh and without mercy
- not keeping covenant by not believing He is the Father of mercies
- not keeping covenant by not believing that God and the Father of Yeshua HaMashiach, the Lord Jesus Christ, is the God of all comfort when he/she is in tribulation
- not living from or receiving the covenant provisions of grace and peace that comes from God the Father and Yeshua HaMashiach, the Lord Jesus Christ

- not keeping covenant—or not receiving the blessings of covenant—by not living from, denying or not believing the truth that the God and Father of Yeshua HaMashiach, our Lord Jesus Christ, has blessed him/her with every spiritual blessing in the heavenly places in Yeshua/Jesus

- not living in covenant by not believing the Father of glory gives him/her the spirit of wisdom and revelation in the knowledge of Him

- not living in covenant by not receiving all that the Father of glory wants to give him/her concerning the spirit of wisdom and revelation in the knowledge of Him

- not keeping covenant by not believing that through Yeshua HaMashiach, Jesus Christ, he/she has access by one Holy Spirit to God the Father

- not living in covenant with his/her Father by not acknowledging the role of the Holy Spirit who gives him/her access to Him

- not living in covenant with the Father by choosing of his/her own accord not to bend the knee to Yeshua/Jesus and confessing with his/her tongue that He is Lord to the glory of God the Father

- not keeping covenant by not giving thanks to the Father and/or not acknowledging that it is He who has qualified him/her to partake of the inheritance of the saints in the light

- not keeping covenant by not receiving and partaking of the inheritance of the saints in the light for which the Father qualifies him/her

- not living in covenant with the Father by not being knit together in love with others in the body of Christ

- not attaining in covenant all the riches of the full assurance of understanding the knowledge of the mystery of God the Father

- not living from the covenant blessings of the Father and Christ in whom all treasures of wisdom and knowledge are hidden

BLESSING ISRAEL

DEAR HEAVENLY FATHER, thank You for being Father to Israel and the Jews. May those of us who follow Yeshua join together in unity with Your people as You are our Father. Please help us to see how much we have in common and build on these truths. Working alongside each other as brothers and sisters with the same Father can accomplish much for the work of Your Kingdom here on earth, amen.

STEWARDSHIP & GROWTH IN SPIRITUAL AUTHORITY

DEAR HEAVENLY FATHER, I turn toward You and seek Your face. As my Father in Heaven, I desire to grow in covenant relationship with You by asking the following questions:

- Are there areas in my life where I have not kept covenant with You by not seeing You as the Father of mercies and God of all comfort in my relationship with You?

- Are there areas in my life where I have not kept covenant with You by not seeing You as the Father of mercies and God of all comfort pertaining to my relationships with others?

- What do I need to remove from my life that keeps me from knowing You better as the Father of mercies and God of all comfort?

- What do I need to add into my life in order to grow deeper in my relationship with You as the Father of mercies and God of all comfort?

- Are there other areas in my life where I do not keep covenant with You from the items listed above in particular where You desire for me to grow in relationship with You?

- What do I need to remove from my life to grow in my covenant relationship with You as my Father?

- What do I need to add in my life to grow in my covenant relationship with You as my Father?

- Pertaining to these items above, what steps do I need to take in order to successfully grow in my covenant relationship with You as my Father?

Blessing

Beloved, as a member of the Royal Priesthood and a child of the Most High God, I bless you to grow in your covenant relationship with Him as your Father in Heaven.

I bless you to keep covenant with your Heavenly Father by believing and declaring there is one God for all people who is Father. I bless you to always live from the truth that He created you for Him and that it is through Him that you live.

I bless you to grow in your covenant relationship with your Heavenly Father as the Father of mercies. May you know that your Father has compassion on you and He longs for you. I bless you to live from the truth that He is the Father of mercies. As you grow in your relationship with the Father of mercies, may you be transformed with your interactions with others as the Lord is the Father of mercies of them .

May you believe and live from the reality in your relationship with your Heavenly Father that He is the God of all comfort. I bless you to receive His comfort when you experience tribulation. As you are blessed with His comfort for you, may His comfort for you overflow to comfort others as they go through tribulation.

I bless you to live in covenant relationship according to the will of God the Father, that you may be delivered from the evil of this age by Yeshua HaMashiach, the Lord Jesus Christ, who gave Himself for your sins.

May you live from the covenantal blessings that the God and Father of Yeshua HaMashiach, the Lord Jesus Christ, has blessed you with by giving you every spiritual blessing in the heavenly places in Christ.

I bless you to live in covenant and believe that the Father of glory gives you the spirit of wisdom and revelation in the knowledge of Him.

May you always live in covenant with the Father of glory and always receive from Him all He desires to give you through the spirit of wisdom and revelation in the knowledge of Him.

I bless you to live in covenant relationship with Yeshua/Jesus. It is through Yeshua/Jesus that you have access to your Heavenly Father through the Holy Spirit. Since you have access to the Father through the Holy Spirit,

I bless you to grow in your covenant relationship with the Holy Spirit.

I encourage you to continually bend your knees to worship Yeshua/Jesus and confess with your tongue that Yeshua HaMashiach, Jesus Christ, is Lord in order to bring glory to God the Father.

I encourage you to keep covenant and give thanks to the Father for qualifying you to partake of the inheritance of the saints in the light. May you keep covenant with the Father by partaking and receiving the benefits of the inheritance of the saints in the light. I encourage you to live in covenant with the Father by being knit together in love with others in the body of Christ.

Beloved, I bless you to live from the covenant blessings from God of all the riches of the full assurance of understanding the knowledge of the mystery of God the Father. May you receive the covenant blessings revealed from the Father and Christ, in whom are hidden all treasures of wisdom and knowledge. I bless you in the name of Yeshua, in the name of Jesus.

Chapter 8

GOD YOUR FATHER #5

Every good gift and every perfect gift is from above, and comes down from the Father of lights, with whom there is no variation or shadow of turning.
—JAMES 1:17

REPENTANCE & REPLACEMENT

AS A MEMBER OF THE ROYAL PRIESTHOOD, please repent of not being in right relationship with your Heavenly Father on behalf of yourself, your generations and your nation for the following and *replace with statements in italics*:

- not keeping covenant with the Father by not doing or saying everything in the name of Yeshua HaMashiach, the Lord Jesus (Col 3:17)
  - *keeping covenant with the Father by doing and saying everything in the name of Yeshua HaMashiach, the Lord Jesus (Col 3:17)*

- not keeping covenant with the Father by not giving Him thanks through Yeshua HaMashiach, the Lord Jesus, in everything that is said or done (Col 3:17)
  - *keeping covenant with the Father by doing and saying everything with thanks to God the Father through Yeshua HaMashiach, the*

Lord Jesus (Col 3:17)

- not receiving from the covenant of the Father by not allowing Him make you increase and abound in love to one another (1 Thess 3:12)
  - *living from the covenant from the Father to increase and abound in love to one another (1 Thess 3:12)*
  - *living in the covenant provision of the Father to establish your heart blameless in holiness before the Father at the coming of Yeshua HaMashiach, the Lord Jesus Christ, with the saints (1 Thess 3:13)*

- not living in covenant relationship with the Father of spirits by not being obedient to Him (Heb 12:9)
- not yielding to His admonition (Heb 12:9)
- not receiving correction from the Father (Heb 12:9)
  - *living in covenant relationship with the Father of spirits by being obedient to Him (Heb 12:9)*
  - *yielding to His admonition (Heb 12:9)*
  - *receiving correction from the Father (Heb 12:9)*

- not living from the covenant blessings that every good and perfect gift comes from the Father of lights (James 1:17)
  - *living in covenant relationship with the Father of lights and receiving and acknowledging that every good and perfect gift comes from Him (James 1:17)*

- not living from the covenant provision of the Father of lights and seeking "good gifts" from other sources (James 1:17)
  - *living from covenant provision of the Father of lights and only seeking good gifts from Him (James 1:17)*

- not living in covenant relationship with God and the Father by having defiled religious worship and religious discipline by not visiting the orphans and widows in their trouble (James 1:27)
  - *living in covenant with God the Father by having pure religious worship and religious discipline by visiting the orphans and widows in their trouble (James 1:27)*

- not living in covenant relationship with God and the Father by having defiled religious worship and religious discipline by not keeping yourself unspotted and irreproachable from the world (James 1:27)
  - *living in covenant with God the Father by having pure religious worship and religious discipline by keeping yourself unspotted and irreproachable from the world (James 1:27)*

- not living in covenant with your God and Father when you bless Him with your tongue and also with it curse men who are made in the likeness of God (James 3:9)
  - *living in covenant with your God and Father when you bless Him with your tongue and also with it bless men who are made in the likeness of God (James 3:9)*

- not recognizing and living in covenant with the God and Father of Yeshua HaMashiach, the Lord Jesus Christ, that it is according to His abundant mercy that has born anew to you to a living hope through the resurrection of Yeshua/Jesus from the dead (1 Pet 1:3)
  - *living in covenant with the God and Father of Yeshua HaMashiach, the Lord Jesus Christ, that it is according to His abundant mercy that has born anew to you a living hope through the resurrection of Jesus Christ from the dead (1 Pet 1:3)*
  - *living in covenant with the Father and living from the hope and*

> *blessing of the inheritance that is to come that is incorruptible and undefiled that is reserved for you in heaven (1 Per 1:4)*
> - *living in covenant with the Father as one who is kept by the power of God through faith for salvation (1 Pet 1:5)*

- not living in covenant relationship with the Father by not calling on Him (1 Pet 1:17)
- not living in the fear of the Lord (1 Pet 1:17)
- not living from knowing you were redeemed with incorruptible things through the blood of Christ (1 Pet 1:18)
  - *living in covenant relationship with the Father by calling on Him (1 Pet 1:17)*
  - *living in the fear of the Lord (1 Pet 1:17)*
  - *living from knowing you were redeemed with the incorruptible and precious blood of Christ (1 Pet 1:18)*

- not living in covenant of eternal life that is with the Father (1 John 1:2)
  - *living in covenant of eternal life that is with the Father (1 John 1:2)*

Please repent of the list above on behalf of yourself, your generations and your nation as to how you have hurt your Heavenly Father or others by these actions.

FORGIVENESS

I CHOOSE TO FORGIVE FROM MY HEART, (person's name), for how he/she did not keep covenant with the Lord as Father by (fill in from list below), which caused injury to myself and/or my loved ones, either now or in the past.

- not keeping covenant with the Father by not doing or saying everything in the name of Yeshua HaMashiach, the Lord Jesus
- not keeping covenant with the Father by not giving Him thanks through Yeshua HaMashiach, the Lord Jesus, in everything that is said or done
- not receiving from the covenant of the Father by not allowing Him make him/her increase and abound in love to one another
- not living in covenant relationship with the Father of spirits by not being obedient to Him
- not yielding to His admonition
- not receiving correction from the Father
- not living from the covenant blessings that every good and perfect gift comes from the Father of lights
- not living from the covenant provision of the Father of lights and seeking "good gifts" from other sources
- not living in covenant relationship with God and the Father by having defiled religious worship and religious discipline by not visiting the orphans and widows in their trouble
- not living in covenant relationship with God and the Father by having defiled religious worship and religious discipline by not keeping himself/herself unspotted and irreproachable from the world
- not living in covenant with your God and Father when he/she blesses Him with his/her tongue and also with it curse men who are made in the likeness of God
- not recognizing and living in covenant with the God and Father of Yeshua HaMashiach, the Lord Jesus Christ, that it is according to His abundant mercy that has born anew to him/her to a living hope through the resurrection of Yeshua HaMashiach, Jesus Christ, from the dead

- not living in covenant relationship with the Father by not calling on Him
- not living in the fear of the Lord
- not living from knowing he/she was redeemed with incorruptible things through the blood of Christ

BLESS ISRAEL

DEAR HEAVENLY FATHER, thank You for keeping covenant with Israel and Your people. Please bless Israel with every good and perfect gift You have for them as the Father of lights, amen.

STEWARDSHIP & GROWTH IN SPIRITUAL AUTHORITY

DEAR HEAVENLY FATHER, I turn toward You and seek Your face. As my Father in Heaven, I desire to grow in covenant relationship with You by asking the following questions:

- Are there areas in my life where I have not kept covenant with You by not seeing You as the Father of lights from whom comes every good and perfect gift? Have I not kept covenant in this area by not accepting gifts from You, not looking to You for good gifts, or looking to others for good gifts?

- What do I need to remove from my life that keeps me from knowing You better as the Father of lights, from whom comes every good and perfect gift?

- What do I need to add into my life in order to grow in knowing You better as the Father of lights, from whom comes every good and perfect gift?

- Are there other areas in my life where I break covenant with You from the items listed above in particular where You desire for me to grow in concerning our relationship?

- What do I need to remove from my life to grow in my covenant relationship with You as my Father?

- What do I need to add in my life to grow in my covenant relationship with You as my Father?

- Pertaining these items above, what steps do I need to take in order to successfully grow in my covenant relationship with You as my Father?

BLESSING

BELOVED, GRACE BE UNTO YOU, and peace, from God our Father, and the Lord Jesus Christ. As a child of the Most High, I bless you to grow in your knowledge and understanding of living in covenant relationship to God the Father.

May all that you do in word and deed be accomplished in the name of Yeshua/Jesus. I bless you to continually give thanks to God the Father through Yeshua/Jesus in all you say and do.

May our God and Father make you to increase and abound in love toward others. In doing so, may He establish your heart blameless in holiness before Himself at the coming of our Lord and Savior with all His saints.

May Yeshua HaMashiach, the Lord Jesus Christ, and our God and Father, who loves you and has given you everlasting consolation and good hope through grace, comfort your heart and establish you in every good word and work.

I bless you to be ready to receive correction from the Father of spirits in order that you may live.

I bless you to acknowledge and receive every good and perfect gift intended for you, which comes down from the Father of lights.

May you be blessed with pure and undefiled religious worship and discipline by visiting the orphans and widows in their trouble. I bless to you to keep yourself unspotted from the ways of the world .

In addition to blessing God the Father with your tongue, may you also bless people who are made in the likeness of God.

May you continually bless the God and Father of our Lord Jesus Christ, who according to His abundant mercy has born anew to you a living hope through the resurrection of Jesus Christ from the dead, to an inheritance that is incorruptible and undefiled, that does not fade away. This is reserved for you in heaven. Blessed are you as one who is kept by the power of God through faith unto salvation ready to be revealed in the last time.

I bless you to call on the Father and to conduct yourselves in the fear of the Lord. I bless you to know that you were not redeemed by corruptible things, such as silver or gold, but with the pure and precious blood of Yeshua HaMashiach, the Lord Jesus Christ.

Beloved, I bless you as a member of the Royal Priesthood and child of the Most High to grow in intimacy of living from the covenant of life and peace made with you by the God and Father of our Lord Jesus Christ. I bless you in the name of Yeshua, in the name of Jesus.

Chapter 9

GOD YOUR FATHER #6

Behold what manner of love the Father has bestowed on us, that we should be called children of God!
—1 JOHN 3:1a

REPENTANCE & REPLACEMENT

AS A MEMBER OF THE ROYAL PRIESTHOOD, please repent of not being in right relationship with your Heavenly Father on behalf of yourself, your generations and your nation for the following and *replace with statements in italics:*

- not living in covenant relationship with the Father by not having fellowship, association or intimacy with Him and His Son Yeshua HaMashiach, Jesus Christ (1 John 1:3)
  - *living in covenant relationship with the Father and having fellowship, association and intimacy with Him and His Son, Yeshua/Jesus (1 John 1:3)*

- not living in covenant relationship with your Father by not going to your advocate, Yeshua HaMashiach/Jesus Christ the righteous, when you sin (1 John 2:1)
  - *living in covenant relationship with your Father and going to your*

advocate, Yeshua HaMashiach/Jesus Christ the righteous, when you sin (1 John 2:1)

- not living in covenant relationship with the Father by loving the world and things of the world (1 John 2:15)
  - *living in covenant relationship with the Father by not loving the world and things of the world (1 John 2:15)*

- not living in covenant relationship with the Father by not having His love in you when loving the world or things of the world (1 John 2:15)
  - *living in covenant relationship with the Father by having His love in you and not loving the world or things in the world (1 John 2:15)*

- not living in covenant relationship with the Father by engaging in the things of the world (1 John 2:16)
  - *receiving the word of Yeshua/Jesus because He is not of the world (John 17:14)*
  - *being in the world but not of the world (John 17:16)*
  - *being sanctified by the truth and word of our Father (John 17:17)*

- not living in covenant relationship with the Father by engaging in the lust of the flesh (1 John 2:16)
  - *living in covenant relationship with the Father by living according to the Holy Spirit and putting to death the deeds of the body (Rom 8:13)*

- not living in covenant relationship with the Father by engaging the lust of the eyes (1 John 2:16)
  - *living in covenant relationship with the Father by making a*

covenant with your eyes to not look lustfully at another (Job 31:1)

- not living in covenant relationship with the Father by engaging in the pride of life (1 John 2:16)
  - *living in covenant relationship with the Father by having the same mind of Christ, who humbled Himself and was obedient to the Father (Phil 2:5-11)*

- not living in covenant relationship with the Father by lying and denying that Yeshua/Jesus is the Christ (1 John 2:22)
  - *living in covenant relationship with the Father by acknowledging the Son (1 John 2:23)*

- not living in covenant relationship with the Father by being antichrist, one who denies the Father and the Son (1 John 2:22)
- The Greek word [G473] for "anti" means, "over against, opposed to, instead of, in place of (something)." Therefore, "antichrist" means, "over against the Messiah, opposed to the Messiah, instead of the Messiah, or in place of the Messiah."
  - *living in covenant relationship with the Father by acknowledging the Son (1 John 2:23)*
  - *living in covenant relationship with the Father by abiding in the truth that leads to abiding in the Son and the Father (1 John 2:24, 27)*

- not living in covenant relationship with the Son and the Father by not having abide in you what you heard from the beginning (1 John 2:24)
  - *living in covenant relationship and abiding with the Son and the Father by having abide in you what you heard from the beginning (1 John 2:24)*

- not living in covenant with the Father by not beholding, not seeing or not perceiving the love He has bestowed on you that you should be called a child of God (1 John 3:1)
  - *living in covenant with the Father by beholding, seeing and perceiving the love He bestows on you that you should be called a child of God (1 John 3:1)*

Please repent of the list above on behalf of yourself, your generations and your nation as to how you have hurt your Heavenly Father or others by these actions.

FORGIVENESS

I CHOOSE TO FORGIVE FROM MY HEART, (person's name), for how he/she did not keep covenant with the Lord as Father by (fill in from list below), which caused injury to myself and/or my loved ones, either now or in the past.

- not living in covenant of eternal life with the Father
- not living in covenant relationship with the Father by not having fellowship, association or intimacy with Him and His Son, Yeshua/Jesus
- not living in covenant relationship with the Father by not going to his/her advocate, Yeshua HaMashiach/Jesus Christ the righteous, when he/she sins
- not living in covenant relationship with the Father by loving the world and the things of the world
- not living in covenant relationship with the Father by not having His

love in him/her when loving the world or the things of the world

- not living in covenant relationship with the Father by engaging in the things of the world
- not living in covenant relationship with the Father by engaging in the lust of the flesh
- not living in covenant relationship with the Father by engaging the lust of the eyes
- not living in covenant relationship with the Father by engaging in the pride of life
- not living in covenant relationship with the Father by lying and denying that Yeshua/Jesus is the Christ
- not living in covenant relationship with the Father by being antichrist—one who denies the Father and the Son
- not living in covenant relationship with the Son and the Father by not having abide in him/her what he/she heard from the beginning
- not living in covenant with the Father by not beholding, not seeing or not perceiving the love He has bestowed on him/her that he/she should be called a child of God

BLESS ISRAEL

DEAR HEAVENLY FATHER, thank You for Your truth that endures to all generations (Ps 100:5). You are Father to Israel and the Jews. As Father You bought them, You made them, and You have established them (Deut 32:6). Please continue to bless them as their Father and Maker. I bless all Your people to know the truth that You are their Father and may this truth endure to all their generations, amen.

STEWARDSHIP & GROWTH
IN SPIRITUAL AUTHORITY

DEAR HEAVENLY FATHER, I turn toward You and seek Your face. As my Father in Heaven, I desire to grow in covenant relationship with You by asking the following questions:

- Are there areas in my life where I have broken covenant with You by not beholding, seeing and perceiving the love You bestow on me that I should be called a child of God?

- What do I need to remove from my life that keeps me from beholding, seeing and perceiving the love You bestow on me that I should be called a child of God?

- What do I need to add into my life in order to behold, see and perceive the love You bestow on me that I should be called a child of God?

- Are there other areas in my life where I break covenant with You from the items listed for repentance in particular where You desire for me to grow in concerning our relationship?

- What do I need to remove from my life in order to grow in my covenant relationship with You as my Father?

- What do I need to add in my life in order to grow in my covenant relationship with You as my Father?

- Pertaining these items repented of, what steps to I need to take in order to successfully grow in my covenant relationship with You as my Father?

Blessing

Beloved, as a member of the Royal Priesthood and child of the Most High, your Heavenly Father desires to have you grow and abound in His love. Everything about the Scriptures speaks of the covenant relationship the Father desires to have with His children. I bless you to grow in wisdom, love and intimacy with the Father and in living in covenant relationship with Him through Yeshua HaMashiach, the Lord Jesus Christ.

I bless you to live in the covenant of eternal life that is with the Father. I bless you to grow in your fellowship, association and intimacy with the Father, His son Jesus Christ and the saints of the Lord.

As you walk with the Lord and continue to mature in His ways, if you do sin, I bless you to remember that you have an Advocate with the Father in Yeshua HaMashiach, Christ Jesus. May you be quick to turn to Yeshua/Jesus and never give into the lies of the enemy that would hinder reconciling your relationship with the Father and Son.

I bless you to live in covenant relationship to the Father by having the courage, focus and steadfastness in order to not love the world or the things in the world. May you always receive the word of Yeshua/Jesus because He is not of the world. I bless you to be in the world but not of the world. May the truth and Word of our Father sanctify you as you live in the world.

While living in the world and not being of the world, I bless you to be strong and courageous in the midst of the world not knowing you. The world cannot know you because it does not know the Father. May you live from the truth that when you acknowledge the Son, you have the Father also.

I bless you to love the Father and have His love abide in you. I encourage you to love the Father and to do His will, for those who do His will abide forever.

I encourage you to live in covenant relationship with the Father by living according to the Holy Spirit and putting to death the deeds of the body. I encourage you to live in covenant relationship with the Father by making a covenant with your eyes to not look lustfully at another. I bless you to live in covenant relationship with the Father by having the same mind of Christ, who humbled Himself and was obedient to the Father. May you continually remain in covenant relationship with the Father by acknowledging the Son.

I bless you to let the truth abide in you, which you heard from the beginning. For in doing so, you will abide in the Father and Son. May you receive the fullness of the promise of eternal life, which He promised.

Beloved, behold what manner of love the Father has bestowed on you, that you would be called children of God. I bless you in the name of Yeshua, in the name of Jesus.

PART 3

THE LORD YOUR HUSBAND

For your Maker is your husband,
The LORD of hosts is His name;
And your Redeemer is the Holy One of Israel;
He is called the God of the whole earth.
—ISAIAH 54:5

As we continue praying through the mountain of family in our nations, we shift our focus from the Lord our Father to our relationship with Him as the Lord our Husband. There are several aspects to the nature of the Lord our Husband. He is our Maker; He is the Lord of Hosts; He is our Redeemer; He is the Holy One of Israel; and He is the God of the Whole Earth. Focusing on the Lord our Husband as the Holy One of Israel fits our purpose of praying for healing for our nations in context of the family, as well as the Lord our Husband and Redeemer.

As the Bride of Christ and members of the Royal Priesthood, it is imperative that we are in right relationship with our King and Bridegroom. The Holy One of Israel is Husband and sovereign ruler over the nation of Israel. Much can be learned in Scripture about how we are to relate to the Lord our Husband that would impact the culture of our families and nations.

Likewise, when we live in right relationship with the Holy One of Israel, we then live in agreement with the covenant of peace the Lord made to the nation of Israel and the Jews.

Let us join together in repenting of how we have sinned individually, generationally and as a nation against the Lord as our Husband, the Holy One of Israel and the Lord our Redeemer.

Chapter 10

THE HOLY ONE OF ISRAEL #1

Thus says the LORD, your Redeemer,
The Holy One of Israel: "I am the LORD your God,
Who teaches you to profit,
Who leads you by the way you should go."
—ISAIAH 48:17

REPENTANCE & REPLACEMENT

AS THE BRIDE OF CHRIST and a member of the Royal Priesthood, please repent of not keeping covenant with the Lord your Husband, the Holy One of Israel, on behalf of yourself, your generations and your nation for the following and *replace with statements in italics:*

- reproaching, taunting, blaspheming, defying, railing and upbraiding the Lord your Husband, the Holy one of Israel (2 Ki 10:22; Is 37:23)
    - the Hebrew word [H2778] translated as reproach means, "to reproach, taunt, blaspheme, defy, jeopardize, rail, upbraid"
- jeopardizing your relationship with the Lord your Husband, the Holy One of Israel by reproaching Him (2 Ki 10:22; Is 37:23)
- blaspheming your Husband, the Holy One of Israel (2 Ki 10:22; Is 37:23)
- raising your voice in exaltation against your Husband, the Holy One of Israel (2 Ki 10:22; Is 37:23)

- lifting up your eyes and exalting yourself against your Husband, the Holy One of Israel (2 Ki 10:22; Is 37:23)
  - *praising and singing to your Husband, the Holy One of Israel (Ps 71:22)*
  - *rejoicing with lips and soul in song to the One who redeemed you, your Husband, your Redeemer (Ps 71:23)*
  - *talking and testifying all day of His righteousness, of the Lord your Husband, the Holy One of Israel (Ps 71:22, 24)*
  - *looking to your Maker and having eyes that respect the Holy One of Israel (Is 17:7)*
  - *glorying in the Holy One of Israel (Is 41:16)*

- provoking Him during wilderness experiences (Ps 78:40)
- grieving Him while in the desert (Ps 78:40)
- tempting God, your Husband, the Holy One of Israel (Ps 78:41)
  - this Hebrew word [H5254] translated "tempt" means, "to test, try, prove, tempt, assay, put to the proof or test"
- limiting the Holy One of Israel, your Husband (Ps 78:41)
- not remembering the power of your Husband, the Holy One of Israel, when He redeemed you from the enemy (Ps 78:42)
- not remembering the power of your Husband, the Holy One of Israel, when He worked His signs in Egypt (Ps 78:43)
  - *remembering the works of the Lord (Ps 77:11)*
  - *remembering the ancient wonders the Lord accomplished (Ps 77:11)*
  - *meditating on all the works of the Lord your Husband, your Maker, your Redeemer, the Lord of Hosts, the Holy One of Israel, the God of the Whole Earth (Ps 77:11, Is 54:5)*
  - *talking of the deeds of the Lord your Husband, your Maker, your Redeemer, the Lord of Hosts, the Holy One of Israel, the God of the*

Whole Earth (Ps 77:11, Is 54:5)

- ◆ *the Lord your Husband, your Redeemer, the Holy One of Israel helps you by making you into a new threshing sledge with sharp teeth (Is 41:14-15)*
- ◆ *rejoicing in the Lord and glorying in the Lord your Husband, the Holy One of Israel (Is 41:16)*
- ◆ *listening to and receiving the instructions from the Lord your Husband, your Redeemer, the Holy One of Israel, as He teaches you to profit (Is 48:17)*
- ◆ *following the Lord your Husband, your Redeemer, the Holy One of Israel, as He leads you by the way you should go (Is 48:17)*
- ◆ *praising the Lord as your Husband and declaring His deeds throughout the earth (Is 12:4, 6)*
- ◆ *singing to the Lord as your Husband for the excellent things He has done (Is 12:5-6)*
- ◆ *shouting because the Lord your Husband, the Holy One of Israel, who is great is in the midst of you (Is 12:6)*

Please repent of the list above on behalf of yourself, your generations and your nation as to how you have hurt the Lord your Husband or others by these actions.

FORGIVENESS

I CHOOSE TO FORGIVE FROM MY HEART, (person's name), for how he/ she did not keep covenant with the Lord as Husband by (fill in from list below), which caused injury to myself and/or my loved ones, either now or in the past.

- reproaching, taunting, blaspheming, defying, railing and upbraiding the Lord his/her Husband, the Holy one of Israel
- jeopardizing his/her relationship with the Lord his/her Husband, the Holy One of Israel by reproaching Him
- blaspheming his/her Husband, the Holy One of Israel
- raising his/her voice in exaltation against his/her Husband, the Holy One of Israel
- lifting up his/her eyes and exalting himself/herself against his/her Husband, the Holy One of Israel
- provoking Him during wilderness experiences
- grieving Him while in the desert
- tempting God, his/her Husband, the Holy One of Israel
- limiting the Holy One of Israel, his/her Husband
- not remembering the power of his/her Husband, the Holy One of Israel, when He redeemed him/her from the enemy
- not remembering the power of his/her Husband, the Holy One of Israel, when He worked His signs in Egypt

BLESS ISRAEL

BLESSED ARE YOU ADONAI, the Husband to Israel. Thank you for making an everlasting covenant of peace with her through Your kindness, mercy and tender affection for Your people. May Israel and Your people sing of Your great works. May they never limit You as her Husband, the Holy One of Israel. I bless them to rejoice with their lips and souls in song to the One who redeemed them, their Husband and Redeemer. As the Lord the Husband of Israel, her Redeemer, the Holy One of Israel, please help her by making her into a new threshing sledge with sharp teeth.

May each one of Your people listen to and receive instructions from You, the Lord their Husband, their Redeemer, the Holy One of Israel, as You teach them to profit and lead them in the way they should go. I pray that all Your people sing to You as their Husband for the excellent things You have accomplished for them. May they shout because the Lord their Husband, the Holy One of Israel, is great in the midst of them, amen.

STEWARDSHIP & GROWTH
IN SPIRITUAL AUTHORITY

DEAR LORD, I APPROACH YOU as the Lord My Husband, the Holy One of Israel, and I turn toward You and seek Your face. As the Bride of Christ, I desire to grow in covenant relationship with You by asking the following questions:

- Are there areas in my life where I have broken covenant or not lived from covenant with You by not acknowledging or understanding Your role as the Lord my Husband as the Holy One of Israel?

- What do I need to remove from my life that keeps me from interacting with You as fitting to Your role in my life as the Lord my Husband as the Holy One of Israel?

- What do I need to add into my life in order to interact with You as fitting to Your role in my life as the Lord my Husband as the Holy One of Israel?

- Pertaining to these items above, what steps do I need to take in order to successfully grow in my covenant relationship with You as my Husband as the Holy One of Israel?

BLESSING

BELOVED, AS A MEMBER OF THE ROYAL PRIESTHOOD and as the Bride of Christ, I bless you to grow in your relationship with the Lord your Husband, the Holy One of Israel.

I bless your heart to be filled with love for the Lord your Husband in order for the words of your lips to praise and sing to Him, the Holy One of Israel. May you never reproach, taunt, blaspheme, defy, rail or upbraid the Lord your Husband, the Holy one of Israel. I bless you to hold the Lord your Husband dear, never jeopardizing your relationship by reproaching Him, the Holy One of Israel.

I encourage you to rejoice with your lips and soul in song to your Husband who redeemed you. I bless you to continually talk and testify all day of the righteousness of the Lord your Husband, the Holy One of Israel.

May your eyes be full of respect as you look to your Husband, your Maker, the Holy One of Israel. I bless you to glory in the Holy One of Israel, your Husband.

I bless you to remove all tendencies to provoke the Lord your Husband during any wilderness experiences you may go through. During the desert times, may you never grieve the heart of your Husband. I bless you to never tempt your Husband, the Holy One of Israel.

May you never place limits on your Husband, the Holy One of Israel. I encourage you to remember and meditate on the ancient works of the Lord your Husband, your Maker, your Redeemer, the Lord of Hosts, the

Holy One of Israel, the God of the Whole Earth.

I bless you to talk freely of the deeds of the Lord your Husband, your Maker, your Redeemer, the Lord of Hosts, the Holy One of Israel, the God of the Whole Earth.

May you find the Lord your Husband, your Redeemer, the Holy One of Israel helping you by making you into a new threshing sledge with sharp teeth.

I bless you to rejoice in the Lord and glorying in the Lord your Husband, the Holy One of Israel.

I bless your ears to listen to and receive instructions from the Lord your Husband, your Redeemer, the Holy One of Israel, as He teaches you to profit. I bless you with courage, discernment and wisdom to follow the Lord your Husband, your Redeemer, the Holy One of Israel, as He leads you by the way you should go.

Beloved, I encourage you to praise the Lord as your Husband and declare His deeds throughout the earth. May you sing to the Lord as your Husband for the excellent things He has done. I bless you to shout with joy because the Lord your Husband, the Holy One of Israel, who is in your midst is great. I bless you in the name of Yeshua, in the name of Jesus.

Chapter 11

THE HOLY ONE OF ISRAEL #2

*For thus says the Lord G*OD*, the Holy One of Israel:*
"In returning and rest you shall be saved;
In quietness and confidence shall be your strength."
—ISAIAH 30:15

REPENTANCE & REPLACEMENT

AS THE BRIDE OF CHRIST and a member of the Royal Priesthood, please repent of not keeping covenant with the Lord your Husband, the Holy One of Israel, on behalf of yourself, your generations and your nation for the following and *replace with statements in italics:*

- provoking your Husband, the Holy One of Israel, to anger by being a sinful nation (Is 1:4)
- provoking your Husband, the Holy One of Israel, to anger by being laden with iniquity (Is 1:4)
- provoking your Husband, the Holy One of Israel, to anger by being a brood of evil doers (Is 1:4)
- provoking your Husband, the Holy One of Israel, to anger by being corrupt children (Is 1:4)
- provoking your Husband, the Holy One of Israel, to anger by forsaking the Lord (Is 1:4)

- provoking your Husband, the Holy One of Israel, to anger by turning away backward from your Husband, the Holy One of Israel (Is 1:4)
  - *For thus says the Lord God, the Holy One of Israel:*
    "In returning and rest you shall be saved;
    In quietness and confidence shall be your strength" (Isaiah 30:15).

- despising, spurning, contemning, and abhorring the law and instruction of the Holy One of Israel, your Husband (Is 5:24)
- participating in self-sabotage by not heeding the law and instructions of how to live in the fullness of provision and the blessings of the covenant of the Lord your Husband (Is 5:24)
  - *"Fear not, you worm Jacob, You men of Israel!*
    I will help you," says the Lord
    And your Redeemer, the Holy One of Israel (Isaiah 41:14).
  - *The Lord your Husband, the Holy One of Israel is also your Redeemer. Please ask Him to redeem you from any consequences of despising His law and instruction that have come down through you or your generations. He takes delight in living in covenant relationship with you. In addition, He can and wants to heal any areas in your life that are the roots of your self-sabotage. The Lord your Husband, Redeemer and the Holy One of Israel will help you.*

Please repent of the list above on behalf of yourself, your generations and your nation as to how you have hurt the Lord your Husband or others by these actions.

FORGIVENESS

I CHOOSE TO FORGIVE FROM MY HEART, (person's name), for how he/
she did not keep covenant with the Lord as Husband by (fill in from list
below), which caused injury to myself and/or my loved ones, either now
or in the past.

- provoking the Holy One of Israel to anger by being a sinful nation
- provoking the Holy One of Israel to anger by being laden with
  iniquity
- provoking the Holy One of Israel to anger by being a brood of evil
  doers
- provoking the Holy One of Israel to anger by being corrupt children
- provoking the Holy One of Israel to anger by forsaking the Lord
- provoking the Holy One of Israel to anger by turning away backward
  from the Holy One of Israel
- despising, spurning, contemning, and abhorring the law and
  instruction of the Holy One of Israel
- participating in self-sabotage by not heeding the law and instructions
  of how to live in the fullness of provision and the blessings of the
  covenant of the Lord

BLESSING ISRAEL

BLESSED ARE YOU ADONAI, THE HUSBAND OF ISRAEL. I bless Israel and
Your people to receive from You as her Husband with these words from
Scripture:

For thus says the Lord God, the Holy One of Israel:
"In returning and rest you shall be saved;
In quietness and confidence shall be your strength" (Isaiah 30:15).

"Fear not, you worm Jacob, You men of Israel!
I will help you," says the Lord
And your Redeemer, the Holy One of Israel (Isaiah 41:14).

Thank You for being Husband to Israel, amen.

Stewardship & Growth in Spiritual Authority

Dear Lord, I approach You as the Lord My Husband, the Holy One of Israel, and I turn toward You and seek Your face. As the Bride of Christ, I desire to grow in covenant relationship with You by asking the following questions:

- Are there areas in my life where I have broken covenant or not lived from covenant with You by not acknowledging or understanding Your role as the Lord my Husband?

- What do I need to remove from my life that keeps me from interacting with You as fitting to Your role in my life as the Lord my Husband?

- What do I need to add into my life in order to interact with You as fitting to Your role in my life as the Lord my Husband?

- Pertaining to these items above, what steps do I need to take in order to successfully grow in my covenant relationship with You as my Husband?

BLESSING

BELOVED, AS A MEMBER OF THE ROYAL PRIESTHOOD and the Bride of Christ, I bless you to develop deeper levels of intimacy and interaction with the Lord your Husband, the Holy One of Israel.

I bless you to never provoke your Husband, the Holy One of Israel, to anger. May you bring Him joy by being a righteous nation, being laden with righteousness, being as a child and receiving the Kingdom as such, and turning your face to the Lord your Husband, the Holy One of Israel.

Beloved, hear the Word of the Lord for you.

> For thus says the Lord GOD, the Holy One of Israel:
> "In returning and rest you shall be saved;
> In quietness and confidence shall be your strength" (Isaiah 30:15).

I bless you to return in all ways to the Lord your Husband, the Holy One of Israel. May you be saved by returning and finding rest in Him. I bless you to find strength in quietness and confidence that comes from the Lord your Husband, the Holy One of Israel.

I bless you to love and embrace the law and instruction of your Husband, the Holy One of Israel, in order to live from the fullness of provision and the blessings contained in the covenant He makes with you as His Bride.

Beloved, I bless you to not fear. May you perceive and receive the help that is yours that flows to you from the Lord your Husband, your Redeemer, the Holy One of Israel. I bless you in the name of Yeshua, in the name of Jesus.

Chapter 12

THE HOLY ONE OF ISRAEL #3

Thus says the LORD, your Redeemer,
The Holy One of Israel:
"I am the Lord your God,
Who teaches you to profit,
Who leads you by the way you should go."
—ISAIAH 48:17

REPENTANCE

AS THE BRIDE OF CHRIST and a member of the Royal Priesthood, please repent of not keeping covenant with the Lord your Husband, the Holy One of Israel, on behalf of yourself, your generations and your nation for the following:

- depending on those who have defeated you (Is 10:20)
- going to Egypt for help, or seeking help from a former or current adversary and/or oppressor (Is 31:1)
- relying on horses, or relying on your own resources (Is 31:1)
- not looking to the Holy One of Israel, the Lord your Husband, nor seeking the Lord to help and rescue you (Is 31:1)
- looking to others to lead you (Is 48:17)

Please repent of the list above on behalf of yourself, your generations and your nation as to how you have hurt the Lord your Husband or others by these actions.

Replacement

As the Bride of Christ and a member of the Royal Priesthood, please replace with the following:

- *never again depending on those who have defeated you (Is 10:20)*
- *depending on the Holy One of Israel, the Lord your Husband, in truth (Is 10:20)*
- *shouting because the Holy One of Israel, your Husband, is great in the midst of you (Is 12:6)*
- *looking to the Lord, your Redeemer, the Holy One of Israel, who helps you (Is 41:14)*
- *looking to your Husband, Redeemer, the Holy One of Israel, who teaches you to profit and leads you by the way you should go (Is 48:17)*

Forgiveness

I choose to forgive from my heart, (person's name), for how he/she did not keep covenant with the Lord as Husband by (fill in from list below), which caused injury to myself and/or my loved ones, either now or in the past.

- depending on those who have defeated him/her
- going to Egypt for help, or seeking help from a former or current

adversary and/or oppressor

- not looking to the Holy One of Israel, nor seeking the Lord to help and rescue him/her
- looking to others to lead him/her

BLESS ISRAEL

BLESSED ARE YOU ADONAI, the Husband of Israel. Thank You for Your faithfulness to Israel and Your people. I pray that they have strength and courage to trust only in You and to never depend on those for help who have defeated them in the past. May they shout because You are Husband to Israel and You are great in the midst of her. As her Redeemer, You have promised to help her. May Israel look to You as You teach her to profit and lead her by the way she should go, amen.

STEWARDSHIP & GROWTH
IN SPIRITUAL AUTHORITY

DEAR LORD, I APPROACH YOU as the Lord My Husband, the Holy One of Israel, and I turn toward You and seek Your face. As the Bride of Christ, I desire to grow in covenant relationship with You by asking the following questions:

- Are there areas in my life where I have broken covenant or not lived from covenant with You by not acknowledging or understanding Your role as the Lord my Husband, the Holy One of Israel?

- What do I need to remove from my life that keeps me from interacting with You as fitting to Your role in my life as the Lord my Husband, the Holy One of Israel?

- What do I need to add into my life in order to interact with You as fitting to Your role in my life as the Lord my Husband, the Holy One of Israel?

- Pertaining to these items above, what steps do I need to take in order to successfully grow in my covenant relationship with You as my Husband, the Holy One of Israel?

BLESSING

Beloved, as a member of the Royal Priesthood and the Bride of Christ, I bless you to go deeper in your relationship with the Bridegroom, the Holy One of Israel.

I bless you with courage and strength to be victorious against the propensity to return to those who have defeated you for help. May you be strong and victorious to break any control former adversaries have over you in order to get you to return to them for help.

I encourage you to let go of any reliance you may have on your own resources. I bless you to only trust the resources of the Lord.

I bless you to depend solely in the Holy One of Israel, the Lord your Husband, in truth.

Beloved, I bless you to only seek the Lord your Husband, the Holy One of Israel, to help and to rescue you. May you only seek the Lord your Husband, the Holy One of Israel, to teach you to profit, for it is He who leads you by the way you should go. I bless you to be discerning to hear His instruction. May you have the courage and wisdom needed to implement all He teaches in order for you to profit. I bless your steps to be firm and established by the Lord your Husband, the Holy One of Israel, so that you may walk in the path ordained by Him. I bless you in the name of Yeshua, in the name of Jesus.

Chapter 13

THE HOLY ONE OF ISRAEL #4

For thus says the Lord GOD, the Holy One of Israel:
"In returning and rest you shall be saved;
In quietness and confidence shall be your strength."
—ISAIAH 30:15

REPENTANCE

AS THE BRIDE OF CHRIST and a member of the Royal Priesthood, please repent of not keeping covenant with the Lord your Husband, the Holy One of Israel, on behalf of yourself, your generations and your nation for the following:

- being rebellious (Is 30:9)
- lying (Is 30:9)
- choosing not to hear the law of the Lord (Is 30:9)
- saying to the seers, "Do not see," referring to not seeing the Holy One of Israel, the Lord your Husband (Is 30:10)
- saying to the prophets, "Do not prophesy to us right things," concerning the Holy One of Israel, the Lord your Husband (Is 30:10)
- saying to the prophets to speak to you smooth and flattering things (Is 30:10)

- saying to the prophets to prophesy deceits regarding the Holy One of Israel, the Lord your Husband (Is 30:10)
- saying to the prophets to get out of the way of the Holy One of Israel, the Lord your Husband (Is 30:11)
- saying to the prophets to turn aside from the path of the Holy One of Israel, the Lord your Husband (Is 30:11)
- saying to the prophets for the Holy One of Israel, your Husband, to cease from being before you (Is 30:11)
- despising this word given in Isaiah 30 (Is 30:12)
- trusting, relying on oppression and perversity and not the Holy One of Israel, the Lord your Husband (Is 30:12)
- replying to the Holy One of Israel's request to return and rest in Him for salvation by saying, "No, for we will flee on horses, and we will ride swift." (Is 30:15-16)

Please repent of the list above on behalf of yourself, your generations and your nation as to how you have hurt the Lord your Husband or others by these actions.

Replacement

As the Bride of Christ and a member of the Royal Priesthood, please replace with the following:

- *responding positively to the Holy One of Israel, the Lord your Husband's words, "In returning and rest you shall be saved, in quietness and confidence shall be your strength." (Is 30:15)*
- *waiting on the Lord that He may be gracious and show favor to you (Is 30:18)*

- *by waiting on the Lord, He will be exalted and from this may He have mercy on you because the Lord is a God of justice (Is 30:18)*
- *blessings that come from the Lord for all those who wait for Him (Is 30:18)*
- *hearing with your ears a word behind you saying from the Holy One of Israel, the Lord your Husband, "This is the way, walk in it." (Is 30:21)*
- *defiling the value of idols and throwing them away as unclean things and saying to them, "Get away!" (Is 30:22)*
- *then the Lord will bring the resources needed for your harvest (Is 30:23-25)*
- *the Lord binding up the bruise of His people and healing their wounds (Is 30:26)*

FORGIVENESS

I CHOOSE TO FORGIVE FROM MY HEART, (person's name), for how he/she did not keep covenant with the Lord as Husband by (fill in from list below), which caused injury to myself and/or my loved ones, either now or in the past.

- being rebellious
- lying
- not keeping the law of the Lord
- saying to the seers, "Do not see," referring to not seeing the Holy One of Israel
- saying to the prophets, "Do not prophesy to us right things," concerning the Holy One of Israel
- saying to the prophets to speak to you smooth and flattering things

- saying to the prophets to prophesy deceits regarding the Holy One of Israel
- saying to the prophets to get out of the way of the Holy One of Israel
- saying to the prophets to turn aside from the path of the Holy One of Israel
- saying to the prophets for the Holy One of Israel to cease from being before him/her
- despising the word given in Isaiah 30
- trusting, relying on oppression and perversity and not the Holy One of Israel
- replying to the Holy One of Israel's request to return and rest in Him for salvation by saying, "No, for we will flee on horses, and we will ride swift" (Isaiah 30:15-16).

BLESSING ISRAEL

BLESSED ARE YOU ADONAI, the Husband of Israel. I bless Israel and all the Jewish people to grow in their knowledge and intimacy with You, the Lord their Husband, the Holy One of Israel. May they respond positively to You, the Holy One of Israel, the Lord their Husband's words, "In returning and rest you shall be saved, in quietness and confidence shall be your strength" (Isaiah 30:15). May Israel and Your people wait on You that You may be gracious and show favor to them. By waiting on You, You will be exalted. And, from this may You have mercy on all Jews because You are a God of justice. All who wait on You are blessed. Please bless the ears of Israel and your people to hear You say, "This is the way, walk in it." Please show them anything that hinders them from knowing You as the Lord their Husband. As they do, please send them the resources needed for their harvest. Please heal their bruises and wounds, amen.

Stewardship & Growth in Spiritual Authority

Dear Lord, I approach You as the Lord my Husband, the Holy One of Israel, and I turn toward You and seek Your face. As the Bride of Christ, I desire to grow in covenant relationship with You by asking the following questions:

- In what areas in my life do I need to return to You as my Husband, the Holy One of Israel?

- What do I need to remove from my life to return to You as my Husband, the Holy One of Israel?

- What do I need to add to my life in order to be faithful in returning to You as my Husband, the Holy One of Israel?

- How would You like to heal my bruises and wounds that hinder me from returning to You as my Husband in these particular areas?

- What steps do I need to take in order to put into practice all You have shown me?

BLESSING

BELOVED, AS A MEMBER OF THE ROYAL PRIESTHOOD, I bless you as the Bride of Christ. May you continue to grow in your relationship and intimacy with the Lord your Husband, the Holy One of Israel.

As the Lord reveals areas in your life that require repentance and returning to Him, I encourage you to respond positively to the Holy One of Israel, the Lord your Husband's words, "In returning and rest you shall be saved, in quietness and confidence shall be your strength" (Isaiah 30:15).

I bless you to wait on the Lord that He may be gracious and show favor to you. By waiting on the Lord, He will be exalted and from this may He have mercy on you because the Lord is a God of justice. All who wait on the Lord are blessed.

I bless you to hear with your ears a word behind you saying from the Holy One of Israel, the Lord your Husband, "This is the way, walk in it" (Isaiah 30:21).

As you remove things in your life that hinder your relationship with the Lord your Husband, I bless you to defile the value of these idols and throw them away as unclean things. May you say to them, "Get away!"

In removing the idols from your relationship with the Holy One of Israel, may you find Him bringing you the resources needed for your harvest.

As you grow in your relationship with the Lord your Husband, the Holy One of Israel, may you receive from Him, binding up the bruises and healing your wounds.

Beloved, I bless you to grow in relationship to the Lord your Husband, the Holy One of Israel. I bless you in the name of Yeshua, in the name of Jesus.

Chapter 14

THE LORD YOUR REDEEMER

"For I know that my Redeemer lives."
—JOB 19:25

THE NAME OF THE LORD OUR REDEEMER along with His names the Lord of Hosts, the Holy One of Israel, the God of the Whole Earth, our Maker, are found together repeatedly in the Old Testament. Isaiah 54:5 connects these names of the Lord with the Lord our Husband. Even though the title of the Lord as Redeemer appears in Scripture less frequently than the Lord of Hosts and the Holy One of Israel, the entire Word of the Lord reveals the nature and character of the Lord our Redeemer. Referencing the Lord our Redeemer in title is revealed to us in the Old Testament. It is interesting to note that Yeshua/Jesus is never referred to as Redeemer in the Greek in the New Testament text. We know He is the Redeemer based on the prophecies of the Redeemer revealed in the Old Testament. In Hebrew, the word [H1350] translated as "redeemer" means, "to redeem, act as kinsman-redeemer, avenge, revenge, ransom, do the part of a kinsman." Yeshua/Jesus is in fact our Redeemer.

Our verses for repentance and replacement refer specifically to the Lord as our Redeemer as referenced in the Old Testament. Tying together the connection of the Lord our Redeemer as the Lord our Husband, we focus on drawing closer in our relationship with our Bridegroom as our Redeemer.

Repentance & Replacement

As the Bride of Christ and a member of the Royal Priesthood, please repent of not keeping covenant with the Lord your Husband, your Redeemer, on behalf of yourself, your generations and your nation for the following and *replace with statements in italics:*

- not living from the truth and reality that the Lord your Redeemer lives (Job 19:25)
  - *knowing and living from the truth and reality that the Lord your Redeemer, the Lord your Husband, lives (Job 19:25)*

- not having the words of your mouth be acceptable to the Lord your Redeemer, the Lord your Husband (Ps 19:14)
  - *having the words of your mouth be acceptable and bring pleasure to the Lord your Redeemer, the Lord your Husband (Ps 19:14)*

- neither having the mediation of your heart being acceptable nor bringing pleasure to the Lord your Redeemer, the Lord your Husband (Ps 19:14)
  - *having the mediation of your heart being acceptable and bringing pleasure to the Lord your Redeemer, the Lord your Husband (Ps 19:14)*

- neither having nor remembering the Lord your Redeemer, the Lord your Husband, as your strength and your rock (Ps 19:14; Ps 78:35)
  - *having and remembering the Lord your Redeemer, the Lord your Husband, as your strength and your rock (Ps 19:14; Ps 78:35)*

- not remembering that the Most High God is your Redeemer and the

Lord your Husband (Ps 78:35; Is 54:5)

- ◆ *remembering that the Most High God is your Redeemer and the Lord your Husband (Ps 78:35; Is 54:5)*

- being afraid and/or forgetting that the Lord your Redeemer, the Holy One of Israel, the Lord your Husband, will help you (Is 41:14)
  - ◆ *not being afraid and remembering the Lord your Redeemer, the Holy One of Israel, the Lord your Husband, will help you (Is 41:14)*
  - ◆ *having the perfect love of the Lord cast out all fear (1 John 4:18)*

- being afraid and not remembering you are redeemed by the Lord your Redeemer, the Lord your Husband (Is 43:1)
  - ◆ *remembering you are redeemed by the Lord your Redeemer, the Lord your Husband (Is 43:1)*

- not hearing the Lord your Redeemer calling you by your name (Is 43:1)
  - ◆ *hearing the Lord your Redeemer calling you by your name (Is 43:1)*

- not knowing you belong to the Lord your Redeemer, the Lord your Husband (Is 43:1)
  - ◆ *knowing you belong to the Lord your Redeemer, the Lord your Husband (Is 43:1)*

- not living from the truth that you were formed from the womb by the Lord your Redeemer, the Lord your Maker, the Lord your Husband (Is 44:2; Is 54:5)
  - ◆ *living from the truth the Lord your Redeemer, the Lord your Maker, the Lord your Husband, formed you from the womb (Is 44:2; Is 54:5)*

- neither knowing nor living from the truth that the Lord your Redeemer's name is the Lord of Hosts, the Holy One of Israel (Is 47:4; Is 54:5)
  - *living from the truth that the Lord your Husband, the Lord your Redeemer's name is the Lord of Hosts, the Holy One of Israel (Is 47:4; Is 54:5)*

- not allowing the Lord your Redeemer, the Holy One of Israel, the Lord your Husband, to teach you to profit (Is 48:17)
  - *allowing the Lord your Redeemer, the Holy One of Israel, the Lord your Husband, to teach you to profit (Is 48:17)*

- not allowing the Lord your Redeemer, the Holy One of Israel, the Lord your Husband, to lead you by the way you are to go (Is 48:17)
  - *allowing the Lord your Redeemer, the Holy One of Israel, the Lord your Husband, to lead you by the way you are to go (Is 48:17)*

- living as though the Lord your Redeemer has great wrath toward you (Is 54:8)
  - *living from the everlasting kindness and mercy the Lord your Redeemer, the Lord your Husband, has toward you (Is 54:8)*

Please repent of the list above on behalf of yourself, your generations and your nation as to how you have hurt the Lord your Husband or others by these actions.

Forgiveness

I choose to forgive from my heart, (person's name), for how he/

she did not keep covenant with the Lord as Husband by (fill in from list below), which caused injury to myself and/or my loved ones, either now or in the past.

- not living from the truth and reality that the Lord his/her Redeemer lives
- not having the words of his/her mouth be acceptable to the Lord his/her Redeemer, the Lord his/her Husband
- neither having the mediation of his/her heart being acceptable nor bringing pleasure to the Lord his/her Redeemer, the Lord his/her Husband
- neither having nor remembering the Lord his/her Redeemer, the Lord his/her Husband, as his/her strength and rock
- not remembering that the Most High God is his/her Redeemer and the Lord his/her Husband
- being afraid and/or forgetting that the Lord his/her Redeemer, the Holy One of Israel, the Lord his/her Husband, will help him/her
- being afraid and not remembering he/she is redeemed by the Lord his/her Redeemer, the Lord his/her Husband
- not hearing the Lord his/her Redeemer calling him/her by his/her name
- not knowing he/she belongs to the Lord his/her Redeemer, the Lord his/her Husband
- not living from the truth that he/she was formed from the womb by the Lord his/her Redeemer, the Lord his/her Maker, the Lord his/her Husband
- not knowing or living from the truth that the Lord his/her Redeemer's name is the Lord of Hosts, the Holy One of Israel
- not allowing the Lord his/her Redeemer, the Holy One of Israel, the

Lord his/her Husband, to teach him/her to profit

- not allowing the Lord his/her Redeemer, the Holy One of Israel, the Lord his/her Husband, to lead him/her by the way he/she is to go
- living as though the Lord his/her Redeemer has great wrath toward him/her

BLESSING ISRAEL

BLESSED ARE YOU ADONAI, the Husband of Israel. I bless Israel and Your people to know and live from the truth and reality that the Lord their Redeemer, the Lord their Husband, lives. May each person remember You as the Lord their Redeemer, the Lord their Husband, as their strength and rock. I pray that all Your people will remember that You as their Redeemer will help them. May each one of Your children hear You calling them by his or her own name. I bless Israel and Your people to live from the truth that the Lord their Husband, the Lord their Redeemer's name is the Lord of Hosts, the Holy One of Israel. Please teach Israel and the Jews how to profit and lead them in the way they are to go. I bless all Jews to live from the everlasting kindness and mercy the Lord their Redeemer, the Lord their Husband, has toward them, amen.

STEWARDSHIP & GROWTH
IN SPIRITUAL AUTHORITY

DEAR LORD, I APPROACH YOU as the Lord My Husband, my Redeemer, and I turn toward You and seek Your face. As the Bride of Christ, I desire to grow in covenant relationship with You by asking the following questions:

- What do I need to remove from my life in order to live from the truth that You as my Husband are my Redeemer?

- What do I need to add to my life in order to live from the truth that You as my Husband are my Redeemer?

- As my Redeemer and the Holy One of Israel, what do You want to teach me in order that I may profit from applying Your instruction?

- What steps do I need to take in order to put into practice all You have shown me?

BLESSING

BELOVED, AS A MEMBER OF THE ROYAL PRIESTHOOD, I bless you as the Bride of Christ. May you continue to grow in your relationship and intimacy with the Lord your Husband, the Lord your Redeemer.

I bless you to know and live from the truth and reality that the Lord your Redeemer, the Lord your Husband, lives.

May the words of your mouth always be acceptable and bring pleasure to the Lord your Redeemer, the Lord your Husband.

I bless the mediation of your heart to continually be acceptable and to always bring pleasure to the Lord your Redeemer, the Lord your Husband.

May you keep in remembrance at all times the Lord your Redeemer, the Lord your Husband, is your strength and your rock.

I bless you to remember and live from the truth that the Most High God is your Redeemer and the Lord your Husband.

I bless you to recall that the Lord your Redeemer, the Holy One of Israel, the Lord your Husband, will help you.

I encourage you to hold in your heart and remember you are redeemed by the Lord your Redeemer, the Lord your Husband.

May your ears be open to hearing the Lord your Redeemer calling you by your name.

I bless you to know and live from the reality that you belong to the Lord your Redeemer, the Lord your Husband.

May you always live from the truth that the Lord your Redeemer, the Lord your Maker, the Lord your Husband, formed you from the womb.

I bless you to live from the reality that the Lord your Husband, the Lord your Redeemer's name is the Lord of Hosts, the Holy One of Israel.

May you hear the Lord your Redeemer, the Holy One of Israel, the Lord your Husband, teaching you to profit.

I bless you to always allow the Lord your Redeemer, the Holy One of Israel, the Lord your Husband, to lead you by the way you are to go.

Beloved, I bless you to live from the everlasting kindness and mercy the Lord your Redeemer, the Lord your Husband, has toward you. I bless you in the name of Yeshua, in the name of Jesus.

PART 4

FAMILY RELATIONSHIPS

OUR FOCUS OF REPENTANCE AND REPLACEMENT in Part 4 covers roles as father, mother, son, daughter, husband and wife as addressed in Scripture. One chapter covers the relationship of brothers and men in the family. The equivelant topic of sisters and women in the family has a few Bible references and were included in other chapters. Though each section refers to a particular role, even if you do not fit the specific one, you are encouraged to still pray these prayers for your generations for the sins of those family members who do fit the role, and on behalf of your nation.

As a reminder, not all of these sins may be applicable to those of us praying through these prayers. They may not even be items that we remember or have knowledge of from our past generations. By repenting of our individual sins and generational sins, we are then clean before the Lord and have the authority to repent on behalf of the sins of our country.

These topics of repentance may include a great deal of pain and remorse. Please know that the Lord has freedom, forgiveness, healing and restoration for you, your generations and your nation.

Following the section of *Repentance & Replacement* is *Forgiveness*. You may be the recipient of the effects of these sins and may need to take time to forgive the individual person in your family, the family members in your generations and the role of that member of the family in your nation in order to facilitate further healing in your life.

Chapter 15

RELATIONSHIP OF FATHERS
WITH CHILDREN

And you, fathers, do not provoke your children to wrath, but bring them up in the training and admonition of the Lord.
—Ephesians 6:4

Repentance & Replacement

As a member of the Royal Priesthood, please repent for not keeping covenant with the Lord as a father on behalf of yourself, your past generations, and your nation by the following and *replace with statements in italics*:

- forsaking your son or daughter (Ps 27:10)
- not loving your child (Prov 3:12)
  - *having love for and compassion on your child (Ps 103:13)*
    - *this Hebrew word [H7355] translated as "compassion" includes meanings, "to love, love deeply, have mercy, be compassionate, have tender affection [for], have compassion"*
  - *loving your child (Prov 3:12)*

- not correcting your son or daughter (Prov 3:12)
- not delighting in your son or daughter (Prov 3:12)
  - *correcting your children (Prov 3:12; Heb 12:7)*
  - *delighting in your child (Prov 3:12)*
    - *the Hebrew word [H7521] translated as "delight" includes meanings, "to be pleased with, be favorable to, accept favorably"*

- withholding inheritance from children (Prov 19:14)
  - *passing along inheritance to children (Prov 19:14)*

- not rejoicing over righteous children (Prov 23:24)
  - *rejoicing over righteous children (Prov 23:24)*

- not delighting in wise children (Prov 23:24)
  - *taking delight in wise children (Prov 23:24)*

- lying with a son who is a close relative (Lev 18:6)
- lying with a daughter who is a close relative (Lev 18:6)
  - *not committing incest (Lev 18:6)*

- as a father-in-law lying with daughter-in-law (Lev 18:15)
  - *not committing adultery (Ex 20:14)*
  - *as a father and father-in-law honoring the marriage bed of son and daughter-in-law (Lev 18:15)*

- having your heart turned away from your children (Mal 4:6)
  - *having love for and compassion on your children (Ps 103:13)*
  - *turning your heart to your children (Mal 4:6)*

- provoking your children to wrath (Eph 6:4)
- exasperating your children (Eph 6:4)

- provoking your children to anger (Eph 6:4)
- not being gentle in giving instruction or correction (Eph 6:4)
- not bringing up children in the exhortation of the Lord (Eph 6:4)
- not inciting, or exciting to action, your children to good deeds (Eph 6:4)
- provoking your children so that they became discouraged and lost heart (Col 3:21)
  - *not provoking your children to wrath (Eph 6:4)*
    - *"provoke" and "wrath" are the same word in Greek [G3949] and include the meanings, "to rouse to wrath, to provoke, exasperate, anger"*
  - *bringing children up in the training and admonition of the Lord (Eph 6:4)*
  - *bringing children up in the exhortation of the Lord (Eph 6:4)*
    - *the Greek word [G3559] translated as "admonition" includes meanings, "admonition and exhortation"*
    - *the English word, "admonition," includes meanings: "Gentle reproof; counseling against a fault; instruction in duties; caution; direction."*
    - *the English word, "exhortation" includes meanings: "The act or practice of exhorting; the act of inciting to laudable deeds; incitement to that which is good or commendable."*
    - *the English word, "incite," means: "The act or practice of exhorting; the act of inciting to laudable deeds; incitement to that which is good or commendable."*

Please consider repenting of how you hurt and injured your relationship with your children by any of the above repentance points that may be applicable.

Forgiveness

I choose to forgive from my heart, (person's name), for how he did not keep covenant of the Lord by (fill in from list below), which caused injury to myself and/or my loved ones, either now or in past generations.

- forsaking you (Ps 27:10)*
- not loving you
- not correcting you
- not delighting in you
- withholding inheritance from you
- not rejoicing over you when righteous
- not delighting in you being wise
- lying with a son and committing incest
- lying with a daughter and committing incest
- a father-in-law lying with daughter-in-law
- having your father's heart turned away from you
- provoking you to wrath
- exasperating you to wrath
- provoking you to anger
- not being gentle in giving you instruction or correction
- not bringing you up in the exhortation of the Lord
- not inciting or exciting you to action and good deeds
- provoking you so that you became discouraged and lost heart

Replacement for father forsaking you
- *allowing the Lord to take care of you (Ps 27:10)*
- *being led by the light and truth of the Lord (Ps 43:3)*

- *this Hebrew word [H571] for "truth" comes from a root word [H539] which includes the meanings, "foster father, foster mother"*

BLESSING ISRAEL

BLESSED ARE YOU FATHER OF ISRAEL AND THE JEWS. Please strengthen all Jewish fathers to have greater capacity of love and compassion for their children than they even know is possible. May their hearts turn toward their children in deeper ways than they currently are doing. Please heal any wounds that exist between fathers and their children. Please bind up the broken hearts that resulted from pain in relationships between fathers and their children, amen.

STEWARDSHIP & GROWTH
IN SPIRITUAL AUTHORITY

Fathers

DEAR LORD, I APPROACH YOU as my Father and I turn toward You to seek Your face. I desire to grow in covenant relationship with You by asking the following questions:

- Are there any wounds that I have from my relationship with my father that need to be healed in order for me to improve in my relationship with my children?

- As a father, what do I need to remove from my life that hinders my growth in my role as an earthly father to my children?

- As a father, what do I need to add to my life in order to grow in my relationship with my children?

- How would You like to heal my bruises and wounds that hinder me from developing a deeper relationship with my children?

- What steps do I need to take in order to put into practice all You have shown me?

Other Family Members

Dear Lord, I approach You as my Father and I turn toward You to seek Your face. I desire to grow in covenant relationship with You by asking the following questions:

- Are there any wounds that I have from my relationship with my father that need to be healed?

- As the recipient of my father's actions, what do I need to remove from my life that hinders my growth due to these old wounds or beliefs?

- As the recipient of my father's actions, what do I need to add to my life in order to grow in restoration and wholeness in my life?

- How would You like to further the healing in my life?

- What steps do I need to take in order to put into practice all You have shown me?

BLESSING

BELOVED, AS A MEMBER OF THE ROYAL PRIESTHOOD, I bless you in your role as a father to your children.

I bless your relationship with the Lord to be full of authenticity and intimacy in order that it overflows into your relationship with your children. I bless you to know the love of your Heavenly Father for you. He tenderly loves you and has great mercy for you. The Lord also gives instructions as to how to keep covenant with Him. I bless you to keep covenant with your Heavenly Father and to know His love for you.

May you always have the courage and strength to respect the marriage covenants of all your family members, including those of your children and daughters-in-law.

I bless you with the wisdom and discernment needed to bring your children up in the training and admonition of the Lord. I bless you to bring your children up in the exhortation of the Lord. May you encourage your children to love and good deeds. I bless you to never provoke your children to wrath.

I bless you to delight in and to be pleased with your children. I bless you to favorably accept your children and to be favorable to them. I encourage you to take delight in having wise children. May you rejoice over righteous children.

Beloved, I bless your love for and compassion on your children to develop to greater expressions. May you always have mercy toward your children and the ability to show tender affection to them. I bless your heart to always be turned toward your children. May you be blessed in order to pass along an inheritance to your children. I bless you in the name of Yeshua, in the name of Jesus.

Chapter 16

RELATIONSHIP OF MOTHERS WITH CHILDREN

"As one whom his mother comforts,
So I will comfort you."
—ISAIAH 66:13a

REPENTANCE & REPLACEMENT

AS A MEMBER OF THE ROYAL PRIESTHOOD, please repent for breaking covenant with the Lord as a mother on behalf of yourself, your generations, and your nation by the following and *replace with statements in italics:*

- lying with a son who is a close relative (Lev 18:6)
- lying with a daughter who is a close relative (Lev 18:6)
  - *not committing incest (Lev 18:6)*

- forsaking your son or daughter (Ps 27:10)
- not loving your child (Prov 3:12)
  - *having love for and compassion on your child (Ps 103:13)*
    - *this Hebrew word [H7355] translated as "compassion" includes meanings, "to love, love deeply, have mercy, be compassionate, have tender affection [for], have compassion"*

- ◆ *loving your child (Prov 3:12)*

- not correcting your child (Prov 3:12)
- not delighting in your son or daughter (Prov 3:12)
  - ◆ *correcting your children (Prov 3:12; Heb 12:7)*
  - ◆ *delighting in your child (Prov 3:12)*
    - ◻ *the Hebrew word [H7521] translated as "delight" includes meanings, "to be pleased with, be favorable to, accept favorably"*

- withholding inheritance from children (Prov 19:14)
  - ◆ *passing along inheritance to children (Prov 19:14)*

- not rejoicing over righteous children (Prov 23:24)
  - ◆ *rejoicing over righteous children (Prov 23:24)*

- not delighting in wise children (Prov 23:24)
  - ◆ *taking delight in wise children (Prov 23:24)*

- not comforting your child (Is 66:13)
  - ◆ *comforting your child (Is 66:13)*

- having generational loathing of your children and being like your mother and your sister in loathing their children (Ezek 16:45)
  - ◆ *having love for and compassion on your children (Ps 103:13)*
  - ◆ *turning your heart to your children (Mal 4:6)*

- having your heart turned away from your children (Mal 4:6)
  - ◆ *having love for and compassion on your child (Ps 103:13)*
  - ◆ *turning your heart to your children (Mal 4:6)*

- provoking your children to wrath (Eph 6:4)

- exasperating your children (Eph 6:4)
- provoking your children to anger (Eph 6:4)
- not being gentle in giving instruction or correction (Eph 6:4)
- not bringing up children in the exhortation of the Lord (Eph 6:4)
- not inciting, or exciting to action, your children to good deeds (Eph 6:4)
- provoking your children so that they became discouraged and lost heart (Col 3:21)
  - *not provoking your children to wrath (Eph 6:4)*
    - *"provoke" and "wrath" are the same word in Greek [G3949] and include the meanings, "to rouse to wrath, to provoke, exasperate, anger"*
  - *bringing children up in the training and admonition of the Lord (Eph 6:4)*
  - *bringing children up in the exhortation of the Lord (Eph 6:4)*
    - *the Greek word [G3559] "admonition" includes meanings, "admonition and exhortation"*
    - *the English word, "admonition," includes meanings: "Gentle reproof; counseling against a fault; instruction in duties; caution; direction."*
    - *the English word, "exhortation" includes meanings: "The act or practice of exhorting; the act of inciting to laudable deeds; incitement to that which is good or commendable."*
    - *the English word, "incite," means: "The act or practice of exhorting; the act of inciting to laudable deeds; incitement to that which is good or commendable."*

Please consider repenting of how you hurt and injured your relationship with your children by any of the above repentance points that may be applicable.

FORGIVENESS

I CHOOSE TO FORGIVE FROM MY HEART, (person's name), for how she did not keep covenant of the Lord by (fill in from list below), which caused injury to myself and/or my loved ones, either now or in past generations.

- lying with a son and committing incest
- lying with a daughter and committing incest
- forsaking you (Ps 27:10)*
- not loving you
- not correcting you
- not delighting in you
- withholding inheritance from you
- not rejoicing over you when righteous
- not delighting in you being wise
- not comforting you
- having your mother's heart turned away from you
- provoking you to wrath
- exasperating you to wrath
- provoking you to anger
- not being gentle in giving you instruction or correction
- not bringing you up in the exhortation of the Lord
- not inciting or exciting you to action and good deeds
- provoking you so that you became discouraged and lost heart

* Replacement for mother forsaking you
- allowing the Lord to take care of you (Ps 27:10)
- being led by the light and truth of the Lord (Ps 43:3)

♦ *this Hebrew word [H571] for "truth" comes from a root word [H539] which includes the meanings, "foster father, foster mother"*

BLESSING ISRAEL

BLESSED ARE YOU FATHER OF ISRAEL AND THE JEWS. Please strengthen all Jewish mothers to have greater capacity of love and compassion for their children than they even know is possible. May their hearts turn toward their children in deeper ways than they currently are doing. Please heal any wounds that exist between mothers and their children. Please bind up the broken hearts that resulted from pain in relationships between mothers and their children, amen.

STEWARDSHIP & GROWTH IN SPIRITUAL AUTHORITY

Mothers

DEAR LORD, I COME TO YOU and I turn toward You to seek Your face. I desire to grow in covenant relationship with You by asking the following questions:

- Are there any wounds that I have from my relationship with my mother that need to be healed in order for me to improve in my relationship with my children?
- As a mother, what do I need to remove from my life that hinders my growth in my role as an earthly mother to my children?

- As a mother, what do I need to add to my life in order to grow in my relationship with my children?

- How would You like to heal the bruises and wounds that hinder me from developing a deeper relationship with my children?

- What steps do I need to take in order to put into practice all You have shown me?

Other Family Members

Dear Lord, I come to You and I turn toward You to seek Your face. I desire to grow in covenant relationship with You by asking the following questions:

- Are there any wounds that I have from my relationship with my mother that need to be healed?

- As the recipient of my mother's actions, what do I need to remove from my life that hinders my growth due to these old wounds or beliefs?

- As the recipient of my mother's actions, what do I need to add to my life in order to grow in restoration and wholeness in my life?

- How would You like to further the healing in my life?

- What steps do I need to take in order to put into practice all You have shown me?

Blessing

Beloved, as a member of the Royal Priesthood, I bless you in your role as a mother to your children.

I bless your relationship with the Lord to be full of authenticity and intimacy that it overflows to your relationship with your children. I bless you to know the love of your Heavenly Father for you. He tenderly loves you and has great mercy for you. The Lord also gives instructions as to how to keep covenant with Him. I bless you to keep covenant with your Heavenly Father and to know His love for you.

I bless you to receive the comfort you need from your Heavenly Father. I bless you to extend the comfort to your children that can only come from a mother.

May all generational loathing of your children and being like the mothers and their sisters in loathing their children in your past generations be broken and not repeated in your life or the generations that follow you. I bless you to have deep love for and compassion on your children.

I bless you with the wisdom and discernment needed to bring your children up in the training and admonition of the Lord. I encourage you to bring your children up in the exhortation of the Lord. May you encourage your children to love and good deeds. I encourage you to never provoke your children to wrath.

I bless you to delight in and to be pleased with your children. I bless you to favorably accept your children and to be favorable to them. I encourage you to take delight in having wise children. May you rejoice over righteous children.

Beloved, I bless your love for and compassion on your children to develop to greater expressions. May you always have mercy for your children and the ability to show tender affection to them. I bless your heart to always be turned toward your children. May you be blessed in order to pass along an inheritance to your children. I bless you in the name of Yeshua, in the name of Jesus.

Chapter 17

RELATIONSHIP OF PARENTS WITH CHILDREN

But the mercy of the LORD is from everlasting to everlasting
On those who fear Him,
And His righteousness to children's children,
To such as keep His covenant,
And to those who remember His commandments to do them.
—PSALM 103:17-18

REPENTANCE & REPLACEMENT

AS A MEMBER OF THE ROYAL PRIESTHOOD, please repent of not keeping covenant with the Lord as a parent on behalf of yourself, your generations and your nation for the following and *replace with statements in italics:*

- withholding son or daughter from the Lord (Gen 22:12, 16)
- loving son or daughter more than the Lord (Matt 10:37)
  - *not withholding son or daughter from the Lord (Gen 22:12, 16)*
  - *loving the Lord more than son or daughter (Matt 10:37)*

- not telling your children and your children's children the mighty things the Lord did in Egypt (Ex 10:2)
- not telling your children and your children's children the signs and miracles the Lord did among them (Ex 10:2)

- *telling your children and children's children the mighty things the Lord did in Egypt (Ex 10:2)*
- *telling your children and children's children the signs and miracles the Lord did among them (Ex 10:2)*
  - *the Hebrew word [H226] translated as "signs" includes the meaning, "miraculous sign"*

- in the Jewish lines of your generations, not observing Passover as an ordinance with your children forever (Ex 12:24)
- in the Christian aspect of your generations, not connecting the Resurrection of the Messiah with Passover, one of the Feasts of the Lord (Ex 12:24)
  - *observing Passover as an ordinance with children forever and celebrating Yeshua/Jesus as the Passover Lamb (Ex 12:24; John 1:29; 1 Cor 5:7)*

- in accordance with the Feast of Unleavened Bread, not observing this and telling your children, "This is done because of what the Lord did for me when I came up from Egypt." (Ex 13:8)
- not connecting the Feast of Unleavened Bread with Passover and Yeshua/Jesus as the Passover Lamb with your children (Mark 14:12)
  - *observing the Feast of Unleavened Bread and connecting it with Yeshua/Jesus as the Passover Lamb with your children (Ex 13:8; Mark 14:12)*

- prostituting, or sex trafficking, your daughter and causing her to be a harlot (Lev 19:29)
- prostituting, or sex trafficking, your son (Lev 19:29)
- the Hebrew word [H2490] translated as "prostitute" includes meanings, "to profane, defile, pollute, desecrate; to profane oneself,

defile oneself, pollute oneself ritually and/or sexually; to be polluted, be defiled; to violate the honor of, dishonor, to violate (a covenant)"

- the Hebrew word [H2181] translated as "harlot" includes meanings, "to be a harlot, act as a harlot, commit fornication, to commit adultery, to be a cult prostitute, to be unfaithful (to God) (fig.)"
  - *not prostituting your daughter (Lev 19:29)*
  - *not causing your daughter to be a harlot (Lev 19:29)*

- not teaching your children the words of the Lord (Deut 4:10)
- not teaching your children to fear the Lord (Deut 4:10)
  - *teaching your children the words of the Lord (Deut 4:10)*
  - *teaching your children to fear the Lord (Deut 4:10; Ps 34:11)*
  - *the mercy of the Lord is never-ending to those who fear the Lord (Ps 103:17)*

- not fearing the Lord and not keeping His commandments leads to things not being well for you and your children (Deut 5:29)
  - *fearing the Lord and keeping His commandments in order that it might be well with you and your children forever (Deut 5:29; Deut 12:28)*

- not teaching the commandments of the Lord to your children (Deut 6:7)
  - *teaching the commandments of the Lord to your children that your days may be prolonged (Deut 6:2, 7)*

- for burning sons and daughters in the fire to Molech and other gods (Lev 18:21; Lev 20:1-5; Deut 18:10; 2 Ki 17:17; Jer 7:31-32; Jer 19:4-6)
- for committing abortion, which is a form of child sacrifice (see above references)

- ◆ *not sacrificing children in fires to Molech and other gods (see above references)*
- ◆ *not committing abortion and protecting the life of the unborn child (see above references)*
- ◆ *in faithfulness sanctifying husband, wife, sons and daughters in holiness (2 Chr 31:18)*

- hating your child by not disciplining him/her (Prov 13:24)
- setting your heart on your son or daughter's destruction by not chastening them (Prov 19:18)
  - ◆ *loving your son or daughter by prompt discipline (Prov 13:24)*
  - ◆ *chastening your son or daughter while there is still hope (Prov 19:18)*
  - ◆ *not setting your heart on your son or daughter's destruction (Prov 19:18)*

- not being in agreement with the work of the Lord in the life of your son or daughter when the Spirit of the Lord is upon them and they prophesy (Joel 2:28)
  - ◆ *blessing the work of the Lord in the life of your son or daughter when the Spirit of the Lord is upon them and they prophesy (Joel 2:28)*

Please consider repenting of how you hurt and injured your relationship with your children by any of the above repentance points that may be applicable.

FORGIVENESS

I CHOOSE TO FORGIVE FROM MY HEART, (person's name), for how he/she did not keep covenant of the Lord in the family as a parent by (fill in from list below), which caused injury to myself and/or my loved ones, either now or in past generations.

- withholding son or daughter from the Lord
- loving son or daughter more than the Lord
- not telling his/her children and his/her children's children the mighty things the Lord did in Egypt
- not telling his/her children and his/her children's children the signs the Lord did among them
- not observing Passover as an ordinance with children forever in the Jewish lines of his/her generations
- not connecting the Resurrection of the Messiah to Passover, one of the Feasts of the Lord, in the Christian aspect of his/her generations
- not observing the Feast of Unleavened Bread and telling his/her children, "This is done because of what the Lord did for me when I came up from Egypt."
- not connecting the Feast of Unleavened Bread with Passover and Yeshua/Jesus as the Passover Lamb with his/her children
- prostituting, or sex trafficking, his/her daughter and causing her to be a harlot
- prostituting, or sex trafficking, his/her son
- not teaching his/her children the words of the Lord
- not teaching his/her children to fear the Lord
- not fearing the Lord and not keeping His commandments which leads to things not being well for his/her children

- not teaching the commandments of the Lord to his/her children
- for burning his/her sons and daughters in the fire to Molech and other gods
- for committing abortion, which is a form of child sacrifice
- hating his/her son or daughter by not disciplining him/her
- setting his/her heart on son or daughter's destruction by not chastening them
- not being in agreement with the work of the Lord in the life of his/her son or daughter when the Spirit of the Lord is upon them and they prophesy

BLESSING ISRAEL

BLESSED ARE YOU ADONAI, the Maker of mankind. I come before You to bless Israel and the Jews in their roles as parents in their relationships with their children. I pray that each one of Your people will not withhold son or daughter from You. I pray that the Jews will remember the mighty things You did in Egypt and will tell them to their children. May they be blessed as they observe Passover as an ordinance with their children. I pray that they will continue to teach their children Your words and to teach them to fear, awe and reverence You. May they receive Your never-ending mercy that is bestowed on those who fear You. I bless Your people to fear You and keep Your commandments that it may go well with them and their children forever. May Your people be strong in protecting the life of the unborn and not passing their children through the fire to Molech and other gods. I pray that the families will sanctify themselves in holiness. May parents love their children and be wise in administering discipline. I bless the families to bless Your work in the life of their sons and daughters when the Spirit of the Lord comes upon them and they prophesy, amen.

STEWARDSHIP & GROWTH IN SPIRITUAL AUTHORITY

Parents

DEAR LORD, I APPROACH YOU and I turn toward You and seek Your face. As a member of the Royal Priesthood, I desire to grow in covenant relationship with You by asking the following questions:

- As a parent, what wounds do I need to be healed from in order to grow in my relationship with my children?

- As a parent, what do I need to remove from my life that hinders me living in right relationship with my children in these areas of repentance?

- As a parent, what do I need to add to my life in order to live in right relationship with my children in these areas of replacement?

- What steps do I need to take in order to put into practice all You have shown me?

Other Family Members

DEAR LORD, I APPROACH YOU and I turn toward You to seek Your face. I desire to grow in covenant relationship with You by asking the following questions:

- Are there any wounds that I have from my relationship with my parents that need to be healed?

- As the recipient of my parent's actions, what do I need to remove from my life that hinders my growth due to these old wounds or beliefs?

- As the recipient of my parent's actions, what do I need to add to my life in order to grow in restoration and wholeness in my life?

- How would You like to further the healing in my life?

- What steps do I need to take in order to put into practice all You have shown me?

Blessing

Beloved, as a member of the Royal Priesthood, I bless you in your role as parent. May you grow deeper in your relationship with your children and may your generations be blessed.

I bless you to have the courage and strength to not withhold your son or daughter from the Lord. I bless you to love the Lord more than your son or daughter.

I encourage you to tell your children and your children's children the mighty things, and the signs and wonders the Lord did in Egypt.

I encourage you to share the connection with your children that Yeshua/

Jesus is the Passover Lamb. May you teach your children that the Feast of Unleavened Bread is connected with Passover and Yeshua/Jesus.

No matter what your financial or life circumstances may be, may you never prostitute or sex traffick your daughter or son, nor cause your daughter to be a harlot.

I encourage you to teach your children the words of the Lord. May you teach them to fear Him, for the mercy of the Lord is never-ending for those who fear Him. I bless your family to fear the Lord and to keep His commandments in order that it might be well with you and your children forever. As you teach the commandments of the Lord, may your days be prolonged.

I bless you with strength and determination to never bow the knee to Molech or other gods by offering your children as sacrifices to them through means such as abortion and child sacrifice. If you have done as such in the past, may you find the Lord's forgiveness and mercy in your life.

In your faithfulness to the Lord, may you sanctify your family in holiness to the Lord.

I bless you to show your love to your son or daughter by giving prompt discipline. May you be blessed with wisdom to discipline as appropriate for each child and situation. I bless you to not set your heart on your son or daughter's destruction. May you chasten your children while there is still hope for them.

Beloved, I bless you to see the work of the Lord being accomplished in the lives of your children. I encourage you to bless the work of the Lord in the life of your son or daughter when the spirit of the Lord comes upon them and they prophesy. I bless you in your role as parent in the name of Yeshua, in the name of Jesus.

Chapter 18

RELATIONSHIP OF CHILDREN
WITH FATHERS

Whoever keeps the law is a discerning son.
—Proverbs 28:7

In this topic of repentance and replacement, there are verses about children obeying parents. These refer to being a child and under the authority of a parent. When a child reaches adulthood and is responsible for their actions, then the adult child is no longer required to obey their parents. Even so, the commandment of honoring one's parents is still applicable. However, please remember no one is to love his or her parents more than loving the Lord. At no time whatsoever in an adult's life, is honoring one's parents supposed to be at the expense of relationship with the Lord (Matt 10:37; Matt 19:29; Luke 9:57-62; Luke 14:26). Yeshua/Jesus himself chose to serve His Father when it meant distinguishing Himself from the wishes of His family (Matt 12:46-50). He did this in an honorable way toward His mother, yet did what was right in serving the Father. It is not honoring of one's parents for an adult child to obey his or her parents at the expense of serving the Lord and loving Him with all his or her heart, soul, mind and strength—it is idolatry.

Repentance & Replacement

As a member of the Royal Priesthood, please repent of not keeping covenant with the Lord in your relationship with your father on behalf of yourself, your generations and your nation for the following and *replace with statements in italics*:

- defiling the bed of your father, lying with your father's wife (Gen 49:4; Deut 27:20)
  - *honoring your father's marriage bed and not lying with his wife (Gen 49:4; Deut 27:20)*
  - *not committing adultery (Ex 20:14)*

- striking your father (Ex 21:15)
- cursing your father (Ex 21:17)
- treating your father with contempt (Deut 27:16)
  - *honoring your father that your days may be long (Ex 20:12)*
  - *loving the Lord your God with all your heart, soul and strength (Deut 6:5)*
  - *departing from evil by the fear of the Lord (Prov 16:6)*

- being stubborn and rebellious toward your father and not obeying him (Deut 21:18)
- not heeding the chastening of your father (Deut 21:18)
  - *being humble and obedient toward your father (Deut 21:18)*
  - *heeding the chastening of your father (Deut 21:18)*

- being stiff-necked as your fathers were (2 Ki 17:14; 2 Chr 30:8; Jer 7:26; Acts 7:51)
  - *confessing your iniquity and the iniquity of your fathers (Lev 26:40)*

- ◆ *yielding yourself to the Lord (2 Chr 30:8)*
- ◆ *entering the sanctuary of the Lord (2 Chr 30:8)*
- ◆ *serving the Lord your God (2 Chr 30:8)*

- not hearing the instruction of your father (Prov 1:8; Prov 23:22)
- not giving attention to understanding from the instruction of your father (Prov 4:1)
- being foolish and not heeding your father's rebuke (Prov 13:1)
- being a scoffer and not listening to rebuke (Prov 13:1)
- being a fool and despising your father's instruction (Prov 15:5)
  - ◆ *giving attention to understanding the instruction of your father (Prov 4:1)*
  - ◆ *being wise and listening to your father's rebuke (Prov 13:1)*
  - ◆ *being prudent and receiving correction (Prov 15:5)*

- being foolish and making your father sad (Prov 10:1; Prov 17:21)
- being foolish and being a grief to your father (Prov 17:25)
  - ◆ *being wise and making your father glad (Prov 10:1; Prov 15:20)*
  - ◆ *loving wisdom which makes your father rejoice (Prov 29:3)*

- sleeping in harvest and causing shame (Prov 10:5)
- not working diligently to bring income and causing shame (Prov 10:5)
  - ◆ *being a wise son and gathering in the proper season (Prov 10:5)*
  - ◆ *working diligently to gather for the family (Prov 10:5)*

- mistreating your father and causing shame and bringing reproach (Prov 19:26)
  - ◆ *treating your father well, which results in bringing honor (Prov 19:26)*

- forsaking your father's friend (Prov 27:10)
  - *respecting your father's friend (Prov 27:10)*

- not being a discerning son or daughter by neglecting the law (Prov 28:7)
- being a companion of gluttons and shaming your father (Prov 28:7)
  - *being a discerning son or daughter and observing the law (Prov 28:7)*
  - *being a companion of the righteous and honoring your father (Prov 28:7)*

- having an eye that mocks your father (Prov 30:17)
  - *honoring your father that your days may be long (Ex 20:12)*
  - *being humble and obedient toward your father (Deut 21:18)*
  - *having an eye that is respectful toward your father (Prov 30:17)*

- robbing your father and saying, "It is no transgression" (Prov 28:24)
  - *honoring your father (Ex 20:12)*
  - *not stealing from your father (Ex 20:15)*
  - *neither lying nor dealing falsely with your father (Lev 19:11)*

- having forefathers who forsook the Lord (Jer 16:11)
- having forefathers who walked after other gods (Jer 16:11)
- having forefathers who served other gods (Jer 16:11)
- having forefathers who worshipped other gods (Jer 16:11)
- not keeping the law of the Lord (Jer 16:12)
- doing worse than your forefathers (Jer 16:12)
- following the dictates of one's own evil heart (Jer 16:12)
- not listening to the Lord (Jer 16:12)
  - *having no other gods before the Lord God (Ex 20:3)*

- ◆ *confessing your iniquity and the iniquity of your fathers (Lev 26:40)*
- ◆ *loving the Lord your God with all your heart, soul and strength (Deut 6:5)*
- ◆ *having the fear of the Lord and allowing Him to show you His covenant (Ps 25:14)*
- ◆ *delighting yourself in the Lord that He may grant you the desires of your heart (Ps 37:4)*

- being like fathers and continuing in evil ways (Zech 1:4)
- being like fathers and continuing evil deeds (Zech 1:4)
- being like fathers and not listening to the prophets to turn from evil ways and deeds (Zech 1:4)
- being like fathers and not hearing or heeding the Lord (Zech 1:4)
  - ◆ *having no other gods before the Lord God (Ex 20:3)*
  - ◆ *confessing your iniquity and the iniquity of your fathers relating to continuing in evil ways and evil deeds and not listening to the prophets (Lev 26:40)*
  - ◆ *loving the Lord your God with all your heart, soul and strength (Deut 6:5)*
  - ◆ *obeying the Lord and receiving the blessings that come as a result from obedience (Deut 28:1-14)*
  - ◆ *following the words of the prophets and turning from evil ways and deeds (Zech 1:4)*
  - ◆ *hearing and heeding the Lord (Zech 1:4)*

- not having a heart turned toward your father (Mal 4:6)
  - ◆ *turning your heart toward your father (Mal 4:6)*

- loving your father more than loving the Lord (Matt 10:37; Luke 14:26)

- *loving the Lord more than loving your father (Matt 10:37; Luke 14:26)*

- giving to the Lord that which is supposed to go to bless your father (Matt 15:5-6; Mark 7:11-12)
  - *giving to your father what is his and not taking from him to give it to the Lord (Matt 15:5-6; Mark 7:11-12)*

- having forefathers who spoke well of false prophets (Luke 6:26)
  - *confessing your iniquity and the iniquity of your fathers of speaking well of false prophets (Lev 26:40)*
  - *receiving a prophet in the name of a prophet (Matt 10:41)*

- being of the father the devil (John 8:44)
- doing the desires of the father the devil (John 8:44)
- speaking forth lies like the father the devil, who is the father of lies (John 8:44)
  - *being of the Lord your Father who bought you, made you and established you (Deut 32:6)*
  - *being a son or daughter of your Father in Heaven by loving your enemy, blessing those who curse you, praying for those who use you and persecute you (Matt 5:44-45)*
  - *standing in truth (John 8:44)*

- not obeying your father when you were a child (Eph 6:1; Col 3:20)
  - *obeying your father as a child, for this is right (Eph 6:1)*
  - *obeying your father as a child pleases the Lord (Col 3:20)*
    - *this Greek word, "teknon" [G5043] in Ephesians 6:1 and Colossians 3:20, refers to a young child, whereas the word "huios" that refers to son in a mature sense is used elsewhere in Scripture*

> ❑   *Yeshua/Jesus is always referred to as the Son "huios" of God*

- murdering your father (1 Tim 1:9)
  - *honoring your father (Ex 20:12)*
  - *not murdering your father (Ex 20:13)*
  - *revering your father (Lev 19:3)*

Please consider repenting of how you hurt and injured your relationship with your father by any of the above repentance points that may be applicable.

FORGIVENESS

I CHOOSE TO FORGIVE FROM MY HEART, (person's name), for how he or she did not keep covenant of the Lord by (fill in from list below), which caused injury to myself and/or my loved ones, either now or in past generations.

- defiling your bed and lying with your wife
- striking you
- cursing you
- treating you with contempt
- lying with your daughter or the daughter of his mother, which is incest
- being stubborn and rebellious toward you and not obeying you
- not heeding your chastening
- being stiff-necked and following your example
- not hearing your instruction
- not giving attention to understanding from your instruction

- being foolish and not heeding your rebuke
- being a scoffer and not listening to your rebuke
- being a fool and despising your instruction
- being foolish and making you sad
- being foolish and being a grief to you
- sleeping in harvest and causing shame
- not working diligently to bring income and causing shame
- mistreating you and causing shame and bringing reproach
- forsaking your friend
- not being a discerning son or daughter by neglecting the law
- being a companion of gluttons and shaming you
- having an eye that mocks you
- robbing you and saying, "It is no transgression"
- having forefathers who forsook the Lord
- having forefathers who walked after other gods
- having forefathers who served other gods
- having forefathers who worshipped other gods
- not keeping the law of the Lord
- doing worse than your forefathers
- following the dictates of one's own evil heart
- not listening to the Lord
- repeating generational sins and continuing in evil ways
- repeating generational sins and continuing evil deeds
- repeating generational sins and not listening to the prophets to turn from evil ways and deeds
- not having a heart turned toward you
- loving you more than loving the Lord
- giving to the Lord that which is supposed to go to bless you
- having forefathers who spoke well of false prophets

- being of the father the devil
- doing the desires of the father the devil
- speaking forth lies like the father the devil, who is the father of lies
- not obeying you when he/she was a child
- murdering his/her father

BLESSING ISRAEL

BLESSED ARE YOU ADONAI, the Maker of Heaven and earth. I come before You to bless Israel and the Jews in their relationships as sons and daughters to their parents. May each son or daughter honor their father and depart from evil by fearing You. I bless them to be discerning sons and daughters by observing the law and instruction given in Your Word. I bless them live from the truth that You, their Father, bought them, made them and established them, amen.

STEWARDSHIP & GROWTH
IN SPIRITUAL AUTHORITY

IF YOU ARE NOT ABLE TO HAVE A RELATIONSHIP with your father, perhaps you may desire to ask these questions relating to your Heavenly Father, or based on relationships with men in authority of whom you may have projected your father wounds onto them.

Dear Lord, I approach and I turn toward You and seek Your face. As a member of the Royal Priesthood, I desire to grow in covenant relationship with You by asking the following questions:

- As a son or daughter, what wounds do I need to be healed from in order to grow in my relationship with my father?

- As a son or daughter, what do I need to remove from my life that hinders me living in right relationship with my father in these areas of repentance?

- As a son or daughter, what do I need to add to my life in order to live in right relationship with my father in these areas of replacement?

- What steps do I need to take in order to put into practice all You have shown me?

Blessing

Beloved, as a member of the Royal Priesthood, I bless you in your role as a son or daughter in relationship with your earthly father. I bless you to turn your heart toward your father. If you do not have an earthly father who is alive or you are not in relationship with him, may you grow in your relationship with Your Heavenly Father.

I bless you to honor the marriage bed of your father, mother, brothers and sisters by not committing adultery or incest with members of your family.

May you always treat your father honorably, never striking him, cursing him, or treating him with contempt. I bless you to have eyes that are respectful toward your father.

I bless you to honor your father that your days may be long. May you depart from evil in your relationship to your father by having the fear of the Lord.

I bless you to be humble toward your father. I encourage you to treat your father well, as it results in bringing honor. May you also respect your father's friend.

I encourage you to give attention to understanding the instruction of your father. May you be prudent in receiving correction that comes from him.

May you be wise that it may bring gladness to your father. I bless you to love wisdom that opens the door for your father to rejoice.

May you be a discerning son or daughter and observing the law and instruction of the Lord. I encourage you to only be a companion of the righteous, thereby honoring your father.

I bless you to never rob from your father, lie or deal falsely with him. May you always love and revere your father, never murdering him either physically, with the tongue or in your heart.

I encourage you to confess your iniquity and the iniquity of your forefathers. May you put off everything from your past generations that is not in alignment with the Lord your God (Zech 1:4). I bless you to have no other gods before the Lord God. May you love the Lord your God with all your heart, soul and strength. May your love for the Lord be greater than your love for your father. In doing so, may you be balanced in your love for the Lord and your father; giving to your father what is his and not taking from him and giving it to the Lord.

I encourage you to obey the Lord and receive the generational blessings that come as a result from obedience. I bless you to yield yourself to the Lord and enter His sanctuary and serve the Lord your God. May you have the fear of the Lord, which then allows Him to show you His covenant. I bless you to delight yourself in the Lord that He may grant you the desires of your heart.

Beloved, I bless you to be of the Lord your Father who bought you, made you and established you. May you be a son or daughter of your Father in Heaven by loving your enemy, blessing those who curse you, pray for those who use you and persecute you. I bless you to always stand in truth. I bless you in the name of Yeshua, in the name of Jesus.

Chapter 19

RELATIONSHIP OF CHILDREN
WITH MOTHERS

"'Every one of you shall revere his mother and his father.'"
—LEVITICUS 19:3

REPENTANCE & REPLACEMENT

AS A MEMBER OF THE ROYAL PRIESTHOOD, please repent of not keeping covenant with the Lord in your relationship with your mother on behalf of yourself, your generations and your nation for the following and *replace with statements in italics:*

- striking your mother (Ex 21:15)
- cursing your mother (Ex 21:17)
- treating your mother with contempt (Deut 27:16)
  - *honoring your mother that your days may be long (Ex 20:12)*
  - *loving the Lord your God with all your heart, soul and strength (Deut 6:5)*
  - *departing from evil by the fear of the Lord (Prov 16:6)*

- being stubborn and rebellious toward your mother and not obeying her (Deut 21:18)
- not heeding the chastening of your mother (Deut 21:18)

- scorning obedience to your mother (Prov 30:17)
  - *being humble and obedient toward your mother (Deut 21:18)*
  - *heeding the chastening of your mother (Deut 21:18)*

- forsaking the law of your mother (Prov 1:8)
  - *not forsaking the law, direction or instruction of your mother (Prov 1:8)*
    - *the Hebrew word [H4148] translated as law means, "direction or instruction"*

- being foolish and grieving your mother (Prov 10:1)
  - *being wise and bringing joy to your mother (Prov 10:1)*

- being foolish and despising your mother (Prov 15:20)
  - *being wise and honoring your mother (Deut 5:16; Prov 15:20)*

- being foolish, which is bitterness to your mother who bore you (Prov 17:25)
  - *being a wise son or daughter (Prov 27:11)*

- chasing away your mother, causing shame and bringing reproach to her (Prov 19:26)
  - *honoring your mother (Ex 20:12)*
  - *revering your mother (Lev 19:3)*

- despising your mother when she is old (Prov 23:22)
  - *honoring your mother (Ex 20:12)*
  - *not despising your mother when she is old (Prov 23:22)*
  - *providing for your mother as needed when she is old (1 Tim 5:8)*

- robbing your mother and saying, "It is no transgression" (Prov 28:24)
  - *honoring your mother (Ex 20:12)*
  - *not stealing from your mother (Ex 20:15)*
  - *providing for your mother as needed when she is old (1 Tim 5:8)*

- loving your mother more than loving the Lord (Matt 10:37; Luke 14:26)
  - *loving the Lord more than loving your mother (Matt 10:37; Luke 14:26)*

- giving to the Lord that which is supposed to go to bless your mother (Matt 15:5-6; Mark 7:11-12)
  - *giving to your mother what is hers and not taking from her to give it to the Lord (Matt 15:5-6; Mark 7:11-12)*

- not obeying your mother when you were a child (Eph 6:1; Col 3:20)
  - *obeying your mother as a child, for this is right (Eph 6:1)*
  - *obeying your mother as a child pleases the Lord (Col 3:20)*
    - *this Greek word, "teknon" [G5043], in Ephesians 6:1 and Colossians 3:20, refers to a young child, whereas the word "huios" that refers to son in a mature sense is used elsewhere in Scripture*
    - *Jesus/Yeshua is always referred to as the Son "huios" of God*

- murdering your mother (1 Tim 1:9)
  - *honoring your mother (Ex 20:12)*
  - *not murdering your mother (Ex 20:13)*
  - *revering your mother (Lev 19:3)*

Please consider repenting of how you hurt and injured your relationship with your mother by any of these repentance points that may be applicable.

FORGIVENESS

I CHOOSE TO FORGIVE FROM MY HEART, (person's name), for how he or she did not keep covenant of the Lord by (fill in from list below), which caused injury to myself and/or my loved ones, either now or in past generations.

- striking you
- cursing you
- treating you with contempt
- being stubborn and rebellious toward you and not obeying you
- not heeding your chastening
- scorning obedience to you
- forsaking your law which means, "direction or instruction"
- being foolish and grieving you
- being foolish and despising you
- being foolish, which is bitterness to you who bore him/her
- chasing you away, causing you shame and bringing reproach to you
- despising you when you are old
- robbing you and saying, "It is no transgression"
- loving you more than loving the Lord
- giving to the Lord that which is supposed to go to bless you
- not obeying you when he/she was a child
- murdering his/her mother

BLESSING ISRAEL

BLESSED ARE YOU ADONAI, the Maker of all people. I bless Israel and Your people in their relationships as sons and daughters to their mothers. May they honor and revere their mothers, for in honoring them may their days may be long. I bless them with being wise and bringing joy to their mothers, amen.

STEWARDSHIP & GROWTH IN SPIRITUAL AUTHORITY

IF YOU ARE NOT ABLE TO HAVE A RELATIONSHIP with your mother, perhaps you may desire to ask these questions relating to your Heavenly Father, or based on relationships with women in authority of whom you may have projected your mother wounds onto them.

Dear Lord, I approach and I turn toward You and seek Your face. As a member of the Royal Priesthood, I desire to grow in covenant relationship with You by asking the following questions:

- As a son or daughter, what wounds do I need to be healed from in order to grow in my relationship with my mother?

- As a son or daughter, what do I need to remove from my life that hinders me living in right relationship with my mother in these areas of repentance?

- As a son or daughter, what do I need to add to my life in order to live in right relationship with my mother in these areas of replacement?

- What steps do I need to take in order to put into practice all You have shown me?

BLESSING

BELOVED, AS A MEMBER OF THE ROYAL PRIESTHOOD, I bless you as a son or daughter in your relationship with your mother. May you grow deeper in your relationship with your mother in ways that are consistent to bringing you long life. If you do not have an earthly mother who is alive or you are not in relationship with her, may you grow in your relationship with your Heavenly Father, for He will take care of you (Ps 27:10).

May you always treat your mother honorably, never striking her, cursing her or treating her with contempt. I encourage you to never chase away your mother causing shame and bringing reproach. I bless you to revere your mother.

May you never despise your mother when she is old. I bless you to take care of and provide for your mother as needed when she is old.

I bless you to be humble toward your mother. I encourage you to treat your mother well, as it results in bringing honor.

I encourage you to give attention to understanding the instruction of your mother.

May you be wise that it may bring joy to your mother. I bless you to be wise by honoring her.

I bless you to never rob from your mother. May you always love and revere your mother. May you never murder her, either physically with the tongue or in your heart. I bless you to provide for your mother as needed when she is old.

Beloved, I bless you to have no other gods before the Lord. May you love the Lord your God with all your heart, soul and strength. May your love for the Him be greater than your love for your mother. In doing so, may you be balanced in your love for the Lord and your mother—giving to your mother what is hers and giving to the Lord what is His. I bless you in the name of Yeshua, in the name of Jesus.

Chapter 20

RELATIONSHIP OF BROTHERS
& MEN WITH FAMILY

*And such were some of you. But you were washed,
but you were sanctified, but you were justified in the
name of the Lord Jesus and by the Spirit of our God.*
—1 CORINTHIANS 6:11

REPENTANCE

AS A MEMBER OF THE ROYAL PRIESTHOOD, please repent of not keeping covenant with the Lord in your relationship as brother or man with your family on behalf of yourself, your generations and your nation for the following:

- uncovering the nakedness of, or lying with, your father's wife's daughter, your sister (Lev 18:11)
- uncovering the nakedness of your father's brother by lying with his wife, your aunt (Lev 18:14)
- uncovering the nakedness of your brother's wife by lying with her, your sister-in-law (Lev 18:16)
- lying with or taking your father's wife (Lev 20:11; Deut 22:30)
- marrying a woman and her mother (Lev 20:14)

- uncovering the nakedness of your mother's sister by lying with her (Lev 20:19)
- uncovering the nakedness of your father's sister by lying with her (Lev 20:19)
- uncovering the nakedness of your uncle by lying with your uncle's wife (Lev 20:20)
- taking the wife of your brother (Lev 20:21)
- lying with your sister, the daughter of your father, which is incest (Deut 27:22)
- lying with your sister, the daughter of your mother, which is incest (Deut 27:22)

As applicable, please take time to repent of how participating in the above items caused pain or injury to others.

Replacement

As a member of the Royal Priesthood, *please replace with the following:*

- *not committing adultery (Ex 20:14)*
- *not committing adultery and/or incest and honoring these relationships (Lev 18:11, 14, 16; Lev 20:11, 14, 19-21)*
- *being washed, sanctified and justified in the name of Yeshua HaMashiach, the Lord Jesus, and the Spirit of our God (1 Cor 6:9-11)*
- *Do you not know that the unrighteous will not inherit the kingdom of God? Do not be deceived. Neither fornicators, nor idolaters, nor adulterers, nor homosexuals, nor sodomites, nor thieves, nor covetous,*

nor drunkards, nor revilers, nor extortioners will inherit the kingdom of God. And such were some of you. But you were washed, but you were sanctified, but you were justified in the name of the Lord Jesus and by the Spirit of our God (1 Corinthians 6:9-11).

FORGIVENESS

IF YOU MAY BE THE RECIPIENT of the effects of these sins listed above, please take the time needed to forgive your brother or other men in your family, in your generations and/or the role of brothers and men in your nation in order to facilitate further healing in your life.

I choose to forgive from my heart, (person's name), for how he did not keep covenant of the Lord by (fill in as needed from list above), which caused injury to myself and/or my loved ones, either now or in past generations.

BLESSING ISRAEL

BLESSED ARE YOU ADONAI, the Father of all mankind. I bless the men and brothers of Israel and the Jews to be faithful in their relationships with all their family members. May they be strong and full of honesty and integrity in their family relationships. I bless them to honor their marriage bed along with the marriage bed of each member of their family, amen.

Stewardship & Growth
in Spiritual Authority

Men and Brothers

Dear Lord, I approach You and I turn toward You and seek Your face. As a member of the Royal Priesthood, I desire to grow in covenant relationship with You by asking the following questions:

- As a man and/or a brother, what wounds do I need to be healed from in order to grow in my relationship with my family?

- As a man and/or a brother, what do I need to remove from my life that hinders me living in right relationship with my family in these areas of repentance?

- As a man and/or a brother, what do I need to add to my life in order to live in right relationship with my family in these areas of replacement?

- What steps do I need to take in order to put into practice all You have shown me?

Other Family Members

Dear Lord, I approach You and I turn toward You to seek Your face. I desire to grow in covenant relationship with You by asking the following questions:

- Are there any wounds that I have from my relationships with the men or brothers in my family that need to be healed?

- As the recipient of the actions of men or brothers in my family, what do I need to remove from my life that hinders my growth due to these old wounds or beliefs?

- As the recipient of actions of men or brothers in my family, what do I need to add to my life in order to grow in restoration and wholeness in my life?

- How would You like to further the healing in my life?

- What steps do I need to take in order to put into practice all You have shown me?

Blessing

Beloved, as a member of the Royal Priesthood, I bless you in your role as man and/or brother in your family.

I bless you to honor the marriage bed of each of your family members. May you be trustworthy to honor and protect the marriage covenants of your loved ones.

I bless you and your family to be sanctified in holiness to the Lord.

Beloved, I bless you with the Word of the Lord for you.

Do you not know that the unrighteous will not inherit the kingdom of God? Do not be deceived. Neither fornicators, nor idolaters, nor adulterers, nor homosexuals, nor sodomites, nor thieves, nor covetous, nor drunkards, nor revilers, nor extortioners will inherit the kingdom of God. And such were some of you. But you were washed, but you were sanctified, but you were justified in the name of the Lord Jesus and by the Spirit of our God (1 Corinthians 6:9-11).

Beloved, I bless you as one washed, sanctified and justified by the name of Yeshua HaMashiach, the Lord Jesus Christ, and by the Spirit of our God.

Chapter 21

RELATIONSHIP OF HUSBAND
WITH WIFE

*Husbands, love your wives, just as Christ also
loved the church and gave Himself for her.*
—Ephesians 5:25

Repentance & Replacement

As a member of the Royal Priesthood, please repent of not keeping covenant with the Lord in your relationship with your wife on behalf of yourself, your generations and your nation for the following and *replace with statements in italics*:

- not leaving your father and mother when joining to your wife (Gen 2:24)
  - *leaving your father and mother when joining together with your wife (Gen 2:24; Matt 19:5; Mark 10:7; Eph 5:31)*

- not stepping in and voiding the vows made by your wife when needed in order to protect her from vows she made that would afflict her soul (Num 30:6-15)
  - *protecting your wife as needed to void any vows she has made that*

may afflict her soul (Num 30:6-15)

- being a former husband to a wife who married a second time and then taking her back and remarrying her after her second marriage (Deut 24:4)

- not being the head of your the wife as Christ is the head of the Church (Eph 5:23)
    - *being the head of your wife as Christ is the head of the Church (Eph 5:23)*
    - *loving your wife as Christ loves the Church (Eph 5:25)*
    - *having the mind of Christ and His humility (Phil 2:5-11)*

- not loving your wife as Christ loved the Church and gave Himself for Her (Eph 5:25)
    - *loving your wife as Christ loved the Church and gave Himself for Her (Eph 5:25)*

- not loving your wife as your own body (Eph 5:28)
- not loving yourself by not loving your wife (Eph 5:28)
    - *loving your wife as your own body (Eph 5:28, 33)*
    - *loving yourself by loving your wife (Eph 5:28)*

- being bitter toward your wife (Col 3:19)
    - *loving your wife as Christ loved the Church (Eph 5:25)*
    - *not being bitter toward your wife (Col 3:19)*

- not rendering affection due to your wife (1 Cor 7:3)
    - *rendering affection due to your wife (1 Cor 7:3)*

- not dwelling with your wife with understanding (1 Pet 3:7)
- not giving honor to your wife (1 Pet 3:7)
- not being together with your wife as heirs of the grace of life (1 Pet 3:7)
  - *dwelling with your wife with understanding (1 Pet 3:7)*
  - *giving honor to your wife (1 Pet 3:7)*
  - *being heirs together with your wife of the grace of life (1 Pet 3:7)*
  - *doing these as listed above in order that your prayers may not be hindered (1 Pet 3:7)*

Please consider repenting of how you hurt and injured your relationship with your wife by any of the above repentance points that may be applicable.

FORGIVENESS

IF YOU ARE THE RECIPIENT of the effects of these sins listed above, please take the time needed to forgive your husband or those in your generations and/or the role of husband in your nation in order to facilitate further healing in your life.

I choose to forgive from my heart, (person's name), for how he did not keep covenant of the Lord by (fill in as needed from list above), which caused injury to myself and/or my loved ones, either now or in past generations.

Blessing Israel

Blessed are You Adonai, the Maker and Creator of the universe. I bless Your people and Israel and their relationships of husbands with their wives. May each husband be filled with Your love for his wife to provide and protect her, amen.

Stewardship & Growth in Spiritual Authority

Husbands

Dear Lord, I approach You and I turn toward You and seek Your face. As a member of the Royal Priesthood, I desire to grow in covenant relationship with You by asking the following questions:

- As a husband, what wounds do I need to be healed from in order to grow in my relationship with my wife?

- As a husband, what do I need to remove from my life that hinders me living in right relationship with my wife in these areas of repentance?

- As a husband, what do I need to add to my life in order to live in right relationship with my wife in these areas of replacement?

- What steps do I need to take in order to put into practice all You have shown me?

Wives

DEAR LORD, I APPROACH YOU and I turn toward You to seek Your face. I desire to grow in covenant relationship with You by asking the following questions:

- Are there any wounds that I have from my relationship with my husband that need to be healed?

- As the recipient of my husband's actions, what do I need to remove from my life that hinders my growth due to these wounds or beliefs?

- As the recipient of my husband's actions, what do I need to add to my life in order to grow in restoration and wholeness in my life?

- How would You like to further the healing in my life?

- What steps do I need to take in order to put into practice all You have shown me?

BLESSING

BELOVED, AS A MEMBER OF THE ROYAL PRIESTHOOD, I bless you in your relationship as husband with your wife.

I bless you to make the transition needed to leave your father and mother when joining together with your wife. I bless you with the wisdom and discernment as how you are to be joined together with your wife and leave your parents while still honoring them.

I bless you with wisdom to know when and how to protect your wife as needed to void any vows she has made that may afflict her soul.

I bless you to be the head and source of your wife as Christ is the head and source of the Church. May you always love your wife as Christ loves the Church and gave Himself for Her. I bless you to love your wife as your own body, for you love yourself by loving your wife.

May you always love your wife and never be bitter toward her. I bless you to have the mind of Christ and His humility toward your wife. May you always be able to render the affection due your wife.

Beloved, I bless you to always dwell with your wife with understanding and giving honor to her. May you live as heirs of the grace of life together with your wife, that by doing so your prayers may not be hindered. I bless you in the name of Yeshua, in the name of Jesus.

Chapter 22

RELATIONSHIP OF WIFE
WITH HUSBAND

An excellent wife is the crown of her husband.
—PROVERBS 12:4

REPENTANCE & REPLACEMENT

AS A MEMBER OF THE ROYAL PRIESTHOOD, please repent of not keeping covenant with the Lord in your relationship with your husband on behalf of yourself, your generations and your nation for the following and *replace with statements in italics:*

- thinking that having children can be used as a means of gaining your husband's love, affection and attention through control, expectation, fantasy and/or manipulation (Gen 29:34, 30:20)
  - *not thinking that your husband will love you more by having children (Gen 29:34, 30:20)*
  - *not controlling or manipulating your husband to love you by having children (Gen 29:34, 30:20)*

- committing adultery while your husband is out of town, or any other time (Prov 7:19)
  - *not committing adultery (Ex 20:14)*

- causing shame to your husband (Prov 12:4)
  - *being an excellent wife is a crown to your husband (Prov 12:4)*

- being a contentious wife (Prov 19:13)
  - *being a gracious woman who retains honor (Prov 11:16)*
  - *being a prudent wife (Prov 19:14)*
  - *opening your mouth in wisdom (Prov 31:26)*
  - *having teachings of kindness on your tongue (Prov 31:26)*
  - *being a woman who fears the Lord (Prov 31:30)*

- having generational loathing of your husband and being like your mother and your sister in loathing their husbands (Ezek 16:45)
  - *being a wife of noble character (Prov 12:4)*
  - *respecting your husband (Eph 5:33)*

- not submitting to your husband as you would submit to the Lord (Eph 5:22)
  - *submitting to your husband as you would submit to the Lord (Eph 5:22)*
  - *submitting to one another in the fear of the Lord (Eph 5:21)*
    - *remembering that husbands are to love their wives as Christ loves the Church and gave Himself for Her (Eph 5:25)*
    - *husbands are to love their wives as their own bodies and is to love his wife as himself (Eph 5:28, 33)*

- not submitting to your husband as is fitting in the Lord (Col 3:18)
  - *submitting to your husband as is fitting in the Lord (Col 3:18)*
    - *submitting yourself to an abusive husband would not be "fitting in the Lord" as the Lord loves the Church and gave Himself for Her*

- not rendering to your husband the affection due him (1 Cor 7:3)
  - *rendering to your husband the affection due him (1 Cor 7:3)*

- not being submissive to an unbelieving husband (1 Pet 3:1)
  - *being submissive to an unbelieving husband so that without a word your husband may be won by your conduct (1 Pet 3:1)*

Please consider repenting of how you hurt and injured your relationship with your husband by any of the above repentance points that may be applicable.

FORGIVENESS

IF YOU ARE THE RECIPIENT of the effects of these sins listed above, please take the time needed to forgive your wife or those in your generations and/or the role of wife in your nation in order to facilitate further healing in your life.

I choose to forgive from my heart, (person's name), for how she did not keep covenant of the Lord by (fill in as needed from list above), which caused injury to myself and/or my loved ones, either now or in past generations.

BLESSING ISRAEL

BLESSED ARE YOU ADONAI, the Maker and Creator of the universe. I bless the wives of Israel and Your people in their relationships with their husbands. May they be excellent wives and be crowns to their husbands (Prov 12:4). May they be gracious women, for in doing so they retain honor. I bless them to be prudent wives and speaking words of wisdom. May they be wives who fear the Lord and are of noble character, amen.

Stewardship & Growth in Spiritual Authority

Wives

Dear Lord, I approach You and I turn toward You and seek Your face. As a member of the Royal Priesthood, I desire to grow in covenant relationship with You by asking the following questions:

- As a wife, what wounds do I need to be healed from in order to grow in my relationship with my husband?

- As a wife, what do I need to remove from my life that hinders me living in right relationship with my husband in these areas of repentance?

- As a wife, what do I need to add to my life in order to live in right relationship with my husband in these areas of replacement?

- What steps do I need to take in order to put into practice all You have shown me?

Husbands

Dear Lord, I approach You and I turn toward You to seek Your face. I desire to grow in covenant relationship with You by asking the following questions:

- Are there any wounds that I have from my relationship with my wife that need to be healed?

- As the recipient of my wife's actions, what do I need to remove from my life that hinders my growth due to these wounds or beliefs?

- As the recipient of my wife's actions, what do I need to add to my life in order to grow in restoration and wholeness in my life?

- How would You like to further the healing in my life?

- What steps do I need to take in order to put into practice all You have shown me?

BLESSING

BELOVED, AS A MEMBER OF THE ROYAL PRIESTHOOD, I bless you in your relationship as wife to your husband.

I bless you to never have or use your children as a means of gaining your husband's love and affection through control, expectation, fantasy and/or manipulation. I bless you to be strong in the love of the Lord for you so that you can release any control you may wish to exert over your husband.

I bless you to be faithful to your husband at all times in your marriage. I bless you with the capacity to render to your husband the affection due him.

May you never be the source of shame to your husband. I bless you to be an excellent wife that is a crown to your husband.

I bless you to always be a gracious woman, for in doing so you retain honor. May you always be prudent and speak words of wisdom. I bless you to have teachings of kindness on your tongue. May you continually be a woman who fears and reverences the Lord.

May you put off all generational curses of loathing of husbands that may have been committed over the years by mothers and sisters. I bless you to be a wife of noble character. I encourage you to respect your husband.

I bless you to submit to your husband as you would submit to the Lord. May both you and your husband submit to one another in the fear of the Lord.

If your husband is not a believer, I bless you to be submissive so that without a word your husband may be won by your conduct.

I bless you to always remember that the Lord is kind and loving. May you always be mindful that husbands are to love their wives as Christ loves the Church and gave Himself for Her. May your husband love you as his own body and loves you as himself.

Beloved, I bless you to submit to your husband as is fitting in the Lord. May you always remember that submitting to your husband as is fitting in the Lord needs to fit in with the Lord loving the Church and giving Himself up for Her. I bless you in the name of Yeshua, in the name of Jesus.

AFTERWORD

"'Well done, good and faithful servant;
you were faithful over a few things,
I will make you ruler over many things.
Enter into the joy of your lord.'"
—MATTHEW 25:21

COURAGE, DETERMINATION, STRENGTH AND TENACITY working together in the power of the Holy Spirit propelled you on a journey of taking a narrow path as you worked through this book. May the Lord bring you—a member of the Royal Priesthood—to broad places in the Kingdom as a result of your diligent labor in *Repentance, Replacement, Forgiveness, Blessing Israel and Stewardship & Growth in Spiritual Authority.*

Well done!

ABOUT THE AUTHOR

RIVKAH ISAACS IS THE FOUNDER of Treasures of Glory Ministries. Her purpose in ministry is to equip the Bride of Christ for victory in the spiritual battle that wages on from ancient times. After many years of application and study in spiritual warfare, Rivkah's series on "The Fruit of the Holy Spirit as Spiritual Warfare" was birthed to come in the opposite spirit of the attacks of the Enemy in order to overcome evil with good (Rom 12:21).

For nearly two years, she led the National Prayer Team for The 2016 Committee, Formerly the National Draft Ben Carson for President Committee, with over 6,000 members who joined together to pray for the healing of the United States of America. Under Treasures of Glory Ministries, Rivkah continues the work in praying for the healing of the nations.